SECULAR PIECES

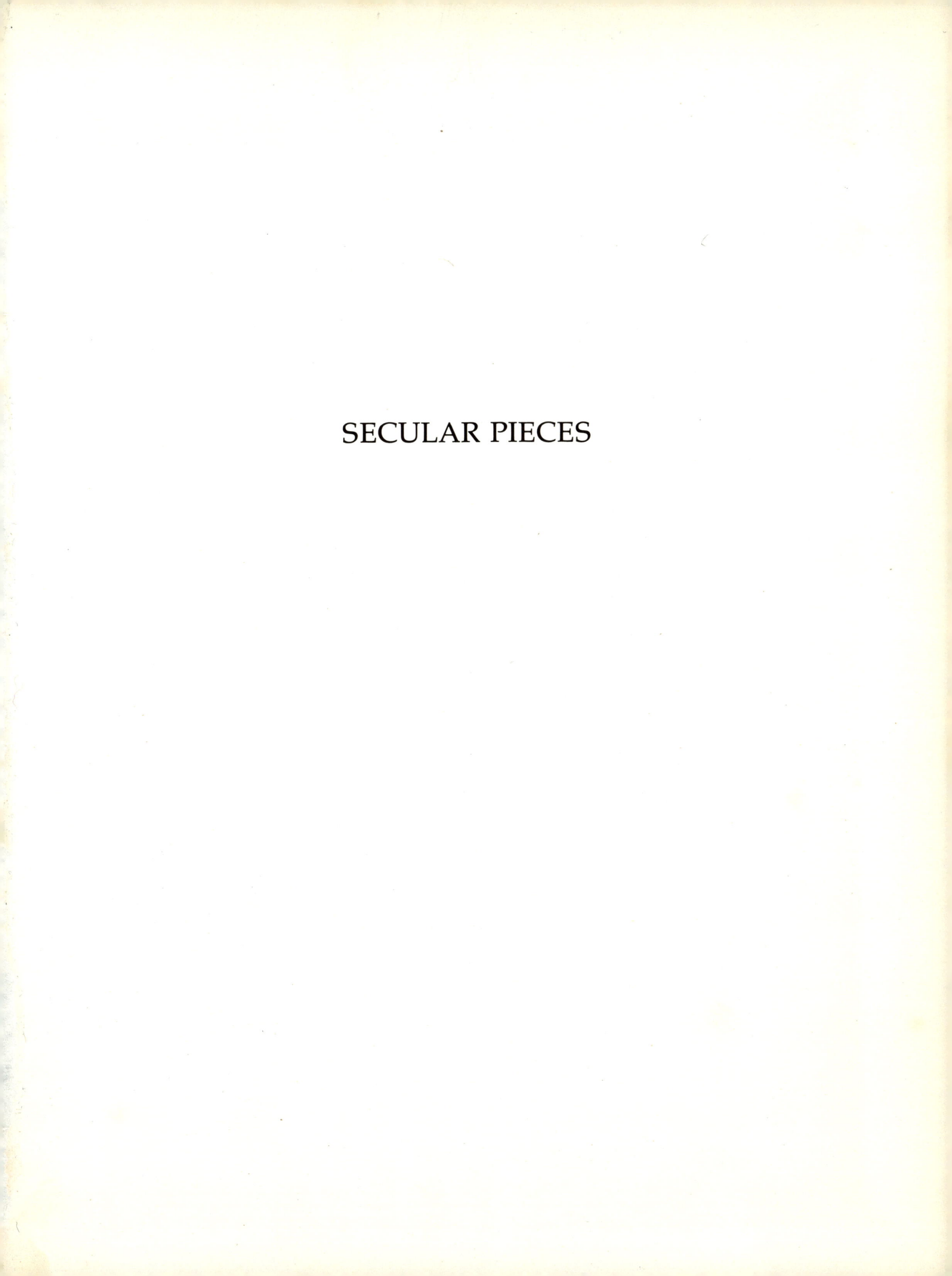

Recent Researches in the Music of the Middle Ages and Early Renaissance is one of four quarterly series (Middle Ages and Early Renaissance; Renaissance; Baroque Era; Pre-Classical, Classical, and Early Romantic Eras) which make public the early music that is being brought to light in the course of current musicological research.

Each volume is devoted to works by a single composer or in a single genre of composition, chosen because of their potential interest to scholars and performers, and prepared for publication according to the standards that govern the making of all reliable historical editions.

Subscribers to this series, as well as patrons of subscribing institutions, are invited to apply for information about the "Copyright-Sharing Policy" of A-R Editions, Inc., under which the contents of this volume may be reproduced free of charge for performance use.

Correspondence should be addressed:

A-R Editions, Inc.
152 West Johnson Street
Madison, Wisconsin 53703

RECENT RESEARCHES IN THE MUSIC OF THE MIDDLE AGES
AND EARLY RENAISSANCE · VOLUME I

Johannes Martini

SECULAR PIECES

Edited by Edward G. Evans, Jr.

A-R EDITIONS, INC. · MADISON

© 1975, A-R Editions, Inc.

Contents

Preface		vii
[1]	Biaulx parle tousjours	1
[2]	Cayphas	3
[3]	Cela sans plus	5
[4]	De la bonne chiere	7
[5]	[Der newe pawir schwantcz]	9
[6]	Des biens d'amours (Version A)	11
[7]	Des biens d'amours (Version B)	13
[8]	Fault il que heur soye	15
[9]	Fortuna desperata	19
[10]	Fortuna d'un gran tempo	21
[11]	Fuga ad quatuor	25
[12]	Fuge la morie	26
[13]	Helas coment (Version A)	28
[14]	Hellas coment anes (Version B)	30
[15]	Il est tel	31
[16]	[Il est tousjours]	33
[17]	J'ay pris amours (Version A)	35
[18]	J'ay pris amours (Version B)	38
[19]	Je remerchi dieu	40
[20]	J'espoir mieulx	42
[21]	La fleur de biaulte	44
[22]	La Martinella	47
[23]	La Martinella pittzulo	50
[24]	Le pouverté	51
[25]	[Malheur me bat]	53
[26]	Nenciozza mia	55
[27]	Non per la	57
[28]	Non seul uno	59
[29]	Per faire tousjours	61
[30]	Que je fasoye	63
[31]	Sans siens du mal	64
[32]	Tant que dieu vosdra	66
[33]	Tousjours bien	68
[34]	Tousjours me souviendra	70
[35]	Tout joyeulx	71
[36]	Tres doulx regart	73
[37]	Vive, vive	75
[38]	[Do si la sol la]	77
[39]	[Re mi fa sol la]	79
[40]	[Re fa sol la la]	81
[41]	[Fa mi re do re]	83
[42]	[Sol me fa sol sol]	85
[43]	[Sol fa mi fa sol]	87
[44]	[Sol la si do si]	89

Other titles found in sources (see Critical Notes):

Dieu damours (= No. 25)

Gardes vous donc (= No. 37)

Groen vint (= No. 12)

Lenchioza mia (= No. 26)

Les bien amore (= No. 6)

Martinella (= Nos. 22, 37 and 43)

O di prudenza fonte (= No. 29)

O intemerata (= No. 5)

Se la sans plus (= No. 3)

Se mai il cielo (= No. 19)

Seruitur (= No. 43)

Preface

In Renaissance Italy, the name of Este commanded respect, if not for might of arms, then for its antiquity and culture. Suffering the usual vicissitudes imposed by men and the confluence of events, the House of Este watched its land holdings stretch and shrink, its powers wax and wane, and its security threatened and solidified many times over during its long rule of Ferrara. In the late Middle Ages, the family had transferred its central authority from the Paduan hills to Ferrara, where it established a rule in 1208 which lasted until 1597. During the Guelf-Ghibelline conflicts, allegiance to the Guelf cause had strengthened the family's political fortunes. By the mid-fifteenth century, the Estes, already celebrated in fabulous legends by poets and chronicles, had acquired the kind of glamour often made possible by wealth and longevity. With such a long established tradition, they could look upon the Medicis of Florence, the Sforzas of Milan and other great ruling families of Italy as relatively young upstarts.

The great age of culture in Ferrara began as early as 1402, when Niccolò III re-opened the university, and continued at least until the death of Ercole I in 1505. For over a century, court life and culture flourished under able leaders: Niccolò III, Twelfth Marquis of Ferrara (1402–1450), and his three sons Leonello, Thirteenth Marquis of Ferrara (1441–1450), Borso, First Duke of Modena and Ferrara (1450–1471), and Ercole I, Second Duke of Ferrara and Modena (1471–1505). Each of these sons, in his own way, proved himself to be a capable although not always wise ruler. As early as 1429, Niccolò III had engaged the great humanist, Guarino Veronese, as tutor in grammar, rhetoric, and poetry for Leonello.[1] By 1436, an inventory of books in Niccolò's library listed some 279 manuscripts, mostly Latin, but also including French (58) and Italian (23) writings.[2] That same year also saw the beginning of a long friendship between Leonello and the celebrated Leon Battista Alberti.

Leonello, who as a "humanist king" might have gladdened the heart of Plato, succeeded his father in 1441. Thoroughly trained in statesmanship, politics, and military art, he also displayed Renaissance versatility as critic, scholar, and poet.[3] Among his personal acquaintances were numbered such artists as Jacopo Bellini, Vittore Pisanello, Andrea Mantegna, Rogier van der Weyden.[4] Equally sensitive to architecture and music, he was also responsible for bringing a choir of singers from France to serve in a beautifully decorated chapel he had ordered built.[5]

Like his predecessor, Borso came to his position well trained in statesmanship and general culture. In 1452, when Emperor Frederick William III of Hapsburg confirmed the title of Duke of Modena and Reggio on Borso, the cities of Ferrara, Modena, and Reggio were witness to spectacular festivities involving music, allegorical representations, processions, feasts, sports and other entertainment.[6] No scholar like his older brother, the new Duke, nevertheless, surrounded himself with humanists and artists, among whom we find the aged Guarino, the Greek scholar Theodore Gaza, and the painters Piero della Francesca, Cosima Tura, and Francesco Cossa. Borso was lavishly praised, and his vanity, of course, was well fed. From among the eulogistic poems current at the time, Antonio Cornazano quotes the following:

> He who would pass from one world to the other,
> Let him hear Pietro Bono play his lute.
> He who would find the heavens opened,
> Let him try the liberality of Duke Borso.
> He who would see paradise on earth,
> Let him see Madonna Beatrice, in a festival (dance).[7]

During the latter years of Borso's rule, his younger brother Ercole strengthened his own position by managing efficiently the duchy of Modena and simultaneously coalescing support for his claims in Ferrara. Shortly before his death, Borso had been summoned to Rome by his old friend and sometime enemy, Pope Pius II, who bestowed upon him the title of Duke of Ferrara. Four months later, Borso died, and Ercole quickly manipulated his own election as the Second Duke of Ferrara on August 20, 1471.

As Ercole I, this youngest of three brothers ruled for thirty-four years. Under him, Ferrara's court life flourished. Aristocracy of blood reaching back centuries was now enhanced by active cultural contact with other noble families in Italy and elsewhere. The University attracted students like Pico della Mirandola and Aldo Manutio, and in 1474 offered forty-five well-paid professors teaching medicine, philosophy, mathematics, astronomy, and jurisprudence. To the court came poets like Matteo Maria Boiardo, Angelo Poliziano, and the young Ludovico Ariosto. Musicians were attracted from various parts of Europe, and wind and string players at Ercole's court were praised by personalities as diverse as Cesare Borgia, Pope Innocent VIII, and Charles VIII, the King of France. According to Bertoni, Ercole himself exhibited skill on stringed instruments, sang well, and owned at least thirteen volumes of song books.[8]

Ercole's fortuitous marriage to Leonora of Aragon, a faithful, intelligent wife, provided him with a strong political ally in King Ferrante of Naples, her father. Their first two children, Isabella (1474–1539) and Beatrice (1475–1497), eventually consolidated other political ties by Isabella's marriage to Gian Francesco Gonzaga, Fourth Marquis of Mantua, and Beatrice's marriage to Lodovico Sforza, Seventh Duke of Milan. Both daughters were cultured, talented, quick-witted, perspicacious and highly intelligent. Isabella, according to contemporary accounts, sang beautifully, played on the lute and clavichord, danced gracefully, collected musical instruments and rare manuscripts, conversed intelligently with scholars and artists, and seemed possessed of an inexhaustible energy which kept her alert to much that happened at court and elsewhere.

As Isabella's tutor in music, the composer Johannes Martini most likely participated in or witnessed some of the rich musical and cultural life at the Ferrara court. More inference than fact, however, surrounds the life of Johannes Martini. The scanty evidence for his activities is scattered in time and place. To the earlier efforts of Valdrighi, Davari, Motta, Bertolotti, and Bertoni, more recent scholars like Barblan, Noblitt, Disertori, Finscher, Morselli, Karp, Brawley, Reese, Wolff, and Lockwood have addressed themselves to the task of collating biographical data and studying the compositions of Martini.[9] Finscher's article, Brawley's dissertation, and the studies by Reese and Lockwood provide excellent summaries of existing information, even though interpretation of evidence varies. For example, Finscher places the composer in the generation of Ockeghem, Reese favors that of Josquin, while Karp views Martini as a "conservative composer of the Josquin generation."[10]

THE COMPOSER

Circumstances of his birth and early life remain obscure, but most scholars have set Martini's birth date as *ca.* 1440. By working backwards from some more firmly established dates, this editor has some doubts about that birth date, which may be almost a decade too early. In his new *Grove's* article (unpublished) on Martini, Lewis Lockwood posits places and dates as follows: *b.* Brabant ?, presumably *ca.* 1440; *d.* Ferrara between late October and late December 1497.

In 1531, Jacques de Meyere names Thomas Martinus and his brothers, Petrus and Johannes, as musicians from Armentières, but he unfortunately provides no birth dates.[11] The Johannes so named is assumed by some biographers to be the composer Martini associated with Ercole I and Isabella d'Este, but no certain connection can be made.

The first document contemporary with Martini's life is the controversial letter dated December 10, 1471, from Ercole I to the Bishop of Constance.[12] Ercole, having heard of the personal integrity, honesty, and excellent musicianship of a priest, Martinus de Alemania, serving in the Cathedral at Constance, asks that the priest be released to him in order to organize a *cappella* at Ferrara. Whether the "Martinus de Alemania" mentioned in this letter, the "Joanne" Martinus named by Jacques de Meyere, and the composer identified today as Johannes Martini are the same person remains an open question. In fact, no evidence exists that the request by Ercole was ever fulfilled. On January 27, 1473, one "Giovanni d'Alemagna," whom most biographers identify as composer Johannes Martini, is installed in the ducal chapel at Ferrara,[13] yet less than two months later, a priest and organist "Iohanni de Alamania" is mentioned in a document found in the *Archivio di Stato* at Milan.[14] In the same year, another register in Ferrara names a "Zohane Martin todesco cantadore compositore."[15] These three may be the same man, but we are not certain.

That the composer Johannes Martini did have an association with the Sforza court in Milan can be established with certainty by a February 28, 1474 ducal passport issued by Galeazzo Maria Sforza to Martini for a trip from Milan to Mantua.[16]

A document of July 15, 1474, shows "Zohanne Martini" among the twenty-two *cantori de' cappelli* employed in the service of the Sforza court in Milan.[17] But a few months later, court records dated November 7, 1474, show that the composer was again in Ferrara.[18] We do not know the circumstances surrounding his employment in Milan and Ferrara, but his salary of five ducats monthly stands at the low end of the salary scale on July 15, 1474. Only one singer received less (four ducats) and four others, including Josquin, earned a salary equivalent to Martini's. In comparison, six singers received ten ducats (double that of Martini), and five others as much as twelve and fourteen ducats.

If the Milan salary be a criterion, it seems unlikely that "Zohanne Martini" could be the same "Martinus d'Alemagna" requested by Ercole from the Bishop of Constance, for the tone of the letter suggests that Ercole was seeking an experienced musician, one to be charged with the responsibility of organizing a *cappella* at Ferrara. The pay level in Milan of July 15, 1474, argues, rather, for a relatively young Martini, hardly a seasoned, mature musician. Martini's long service at Ferrara begins for certain with his departure from Milan in that year; it may have begun, of course, as early as January 27, 1473, with interruptions, if "Giovanni d'Alemagna" and Martini are identical.

If we take into account all the possible references, we find that his given name and surname appear in various spellings, among others, as Johannes, Johane, Jannes, Joanni, Zohanne, Giovanni, Martini, Martino, Martinus, with additional identifications as "de Barbante," "tedescho," "d'Alemagna," and so on. While identity problems of his early life have not been solved, by 1480, "Johannes Martini" had acquired some measure of fame, for that name appears in a Spanish treatise which names eleven of the most illustrious fifteenth-century composers.[19] By linking Martini's name with composers like Dunstable, Dufay, Ockeghem, Binchois, and Busnois, the anonymous author of the Escorial manuscript associates him with well-known musicians. If Martini were born about 1440, the 1480 treatise would find him a mature forty, taking his proper seat in that pantheon of composers. But then the Milan *cantori de cappelli* list of 1474 makes him a thirty-four year old musician with a meager salary, who, six years later, suddenly rises to enough fame to be recognized in a treatise geographically remote from the center of his activity. Were he born about 1450, we can better understand the low salary of a composer who developed rapidly in his late twenties, due in part to providential appointments and innate talent. Even though the pay scale offered musicians by the Sforzas was generally low, Martini in 1474 was at the low end of that low scale, a strong argument for considering him young and relatively inexperienced. Mention of Martini in that Escorial document most probably resulted from his connection with the Este family. As early as 1444, Leonello d'Este had taken as his second wife Maria of Aragon, daughter of Alfonso V, King of Naples; later in 1473, Ercole took as his bride Leonora of Aragon, daughter of Ferrante. These family relations between the daughter of Alfonso "the Magnanimous" and Alfonso's son Ferrante, both of whom ruled over the Aragonese Mediterranean empire, and the Este family obviously resulted in many Spanish contacts through their courts in Naples. Martini's name could easily have been passed on to the anonymous writer of the treatise by these court connections.

During the years following his initial commitment to Duke Ercole, Martini firmly established himself as a musician of some consequence at home and elsewhere. Records either indicate or suggest that he was sent by the Duke on various missions, as part of a courtly retinue accompanying one of the Estensi, or on his own, to Rome, Naples, Modena, Mantua, Florence, and other Italian cities as well as to parts of Hungary, Austria, and Germany.[20]

Beginning in 1489, and continuing into 1492, numerous letters have been preserved which either refer to Martini by name or were actually written by the composer himself.[21] Martini knew Paul Hofhaimer, who in the service of Emperor Maximilian I became one of the most distinguished organists of the time. On September 26, 1489, when Hofhaimer was only twenty years old, Queen Beatrice of Hungary asked her brother-in-law Ercole to intercede on her behalf; she wanted to secure Hofhaimer's services.[22] Toward this end, she probably hoped to use the friendship between the two musicians to good advantage. From her letter it is evident that Queen Beatrice, herself thoroughly trained in music as a child in Naples by the renowned Tinctoris, knew Martini personally or by name. The letter also suggests that Martini had a sufficient reputation to serve as an effective agent, and that the older composer being experienced in court life as well as music, might well persuade the young organist to quit the service of Archduke Sigismund of the Tyrol in favor of the Hungarian court. Time and events conspired to obviate the assignments: Hofhaimer joined the service of Maximilian, the King of Hungary died, and the Queen found herself embroiled in the political aftermath.

Martini's employment with Duke Ercole and his close ties with the young Isabella d'Este, whom he served as musical tutor, no doubt helped to promote his name in musical and courtly circles. Both Isabella d'Este and her younger sister Beatrice must have had many contacts with Martini during their formative years in Ferrara, for both daughters were generously endowed with musical talent. That a close relationship between Martini and Isabella existed can be glimpsed through a number of extant letters. During the late 1470's and 1480's, while Isabella was growing up in Ferrara, little concrete documentary evidence of their relationship remains, since they would have had little occasion to communicate in writing. But after the young girl, not quite sixteen, left home and arrived in Mantua on February 15, 1490, to become the bride of Gian Francesco Gonzaga, letters exchanged between the composer and the new Marchioness of Mantua reveal that Martini continued to be instrumental in the musical training of his young student. In September, 1490, he writes:

> Most illustrious and powerful lady, our most illustrious Duke has told me and commanded me that I ought to come to your ladyship for several days to teach your

ladyship to sing, and I will do it most willingly and with good heart. But since time partly presses me to provide for the needs of my house and partly for other urgent necessities, I beg and entreat your ladyship that she be contented to wait for a fortnight so that I can provide for my needs, and then I will come quickly to your ladyship and will satisfy you as much as I can, and I very willingly await the reply of your ladyship and commend myself a thousand times to you. Farewell.[23]

The next spring Martini sends a song which he recommends for her practice and recreation:

Most illustrious and excellent marchioness, etc. I am sending a song to your ladyship to provide you some recreation and to recommend that your ladyship ought to sing it frequently in order to take good advantage of the practice [it affords]. Always I commend myself to your ladyship. Dated at Ferrara the 18th day of April, 1491.[24]

In other letters, discussion centers around the availability, quality, and behavior (sometimes questionable) of singers. The generally familiar tone suggests that Martini and Isabella remained on friendly terms, probably until the composer's death, which took place, according to Lewis Lockwood, between late October and late December, 1497.[25]

WORKS AND SOURCES

If we are to judge from the geographical range of manuscripts and prints in which his music can be found, Martini seems to have enjoyed a not inconsiderable reputation during his lifetime, for his secular works are found in important Italian manuscripts, especially Florence Banco Rari 229 and Rome Casanatense 2856, as well as more distant ones in Segovia, Seville, Paris, Munich, Jena. Other secular pieces are also located in the Glogauer Liederbuch and in early sixteenth-century publications of Petrucci and Formschneider. Italian sources for his sacred music come from Verona, Milan, Trent, Lucca, Modena, and the Vatican; two principal sources outside Italy are the Munich Ms. 3154 and Jena Ms. 32.

Viewing his significance from another angle, we find that Martini must have had some contact or association with many prominent musicians of his time: Josquin des Prez, Loyset Compère, Alexander Agricola, Isaac, Gaspar van Weerbecke, Paul Hofhaimer, and Jacob Obrecht. With some of these, like Josquin and Compère, he had served as a fellow musician in Milan; others, like Obrecht, he most likely met during his long service under Duke Ercole I. Isaac and Martini were probably instrumental in compiling the Casanatense manuscript.

A third aspect relating to his importance stems from the qualitative level of the music he wrote. While its expressive power may not equal that of Josquin, his music does compare favorably in technical skill and craftsmanship to that of other composers of his day. He was, in other words, a competent composer, well versed in his art.

Martini's output as a composer includes Masses, Magnificats, motets, hymns, and secular pieces. Subsequent volumes in this series will present the sacred music, which in sheer bulk exceeds by far the secular music contained in this first volume. Until the complete works of Martini and his contemporaries have been made available for detailed, comparative study, some of his compositions must remain as *opera dubia*. Generally speaking, this editor intends to include doubtful compositions with the hope that scholars may subsequently expunge or authenticate Martini's name, as the case may be. Given this qualification, I enumerate fourteen Masses, six Magnificats, nine motets, and the present set of forty-four secular pieces. One source, Modena Ms. a.M.1, 11–12, contains additional sacred music in the form of hymns and other music for double chorus, with attributions to Martini and Giovanni Brebis, another musician of the chapel in Ferrara. Four or more volumes will be required to print the Masses and other sacred music, for his entire output is heavily weighted in that direction.

Of the forty-four secular pieces included in the edition, twenty-five are found in one source only, another nine in two sources, and the remaining ten in from three to twelve sources. Using numbers assigned to pieces in the table of contents of this edition and the abbreviations of source names listed in the Critical Notes, the following table graphically illustrates the distribution of pieces found in more than two sources:

Source	22	6	25	19	43	5	12	29	32	37
Flo 229	X	X	X	X	X	X	X	X	X	X
Casa	X	X	X	X		X	X	X	X	
Form	X	X	X	X	X					
G XIII.27	X	X	X		X					
Verona	X			X				X	X	
Q 16	X	X	X							
Q 18		X	X							
Flo 178		X		X						
Segovia							X	X		
Seville	X									X
Glogauer	X					X				
Flo 27		X								
Flo 121		X								
Perugia		X								
Canti A			X							
St. Gall			X							
Egenolff			X							
Trent 89	X									
Trent 91	X									
Basel	X									
Paris	X									
Paris 676					X					

Reading from left to right, we find *La Martinella* (No. 22) with twelve, *Des biens d'amour* (No. 6) with ten, and the problematical *Malheur me bat* (No. 25) with nine sources in that order of frequency. These are followed by *Je remerchi dieu* (No. 19) with five, the doubtful *Sol fa mi fa sol* (No. 43) with five, and the remaining five pieces (in order, *Der newe pawir schwantcz*, *Fuge la morie*, *Per faire tousjours*, *Tant que dieu vosdra*, and *Vive, vive*) with three sources. *La Martinella*'s popularity is attested not only by the number of diverse and scattered sources, but also by its attractiveness to at least three other composers, one of whom, Isaac, borrows freely from Martini in his two settings of *La Martinella*.[26] Martini himself must have been fond of his own piece, for sections of the chanson permeate his lengthy *Missa La Martinella*.[27] In addition, three other Martini pieces bear the incipit "Martinella": *La Martinella pittzulo*, *Vive, vive* (found as *Martinella* in Florence Banco Rari 229), the doubtful *Sol fa mi fa sol* in Casanatense 2856 (f. 138'–140) (found as *La Martinella* in Rome Cappella Giulia XIII.27, f. 68'–69). Two others, *Biaulx parle tousjours* and *Fuge la morie*, open with slight modifications of the *Martinella* head motive. On other occasions he did not hesitate to borrow on pre-existing materials from other sources: *Fortuna desperata*, *Fortuna d'un gran tempo*, *J'ay pris amours*, and *Nenciozza mia*. Of these, it should be observed that the last three are pieces for which texts from other sources have been found. His "si placet" Bassus to *Cela sans plus* constitutes more of a grafting process than a borrowing.

The secular pieces are found in twenty-four different sources if we include all works to which Martini's name can be linked. The number of possible attributions found in each source is given below.

(26) Rome, Biblioteca Casanatense, Ms. 2856
(24) Florence, Biblioteca Nazionale Centrale, Ms. Banco Rari 229 (*olim* Magl. XIX.59)
(6) Verona, Biblioteca Capitolare, Cod. Mus. 757
(5) Formschneider, *Trium vocum carmina*, Nuremberg, 1538 (RISM 1538[9])
(4) Bologna, Civico Museo Bibliografico Musicale, Ms. Q 16 (*olim* 109)
(4) Petrucci, *Canti C. numero cento cinquanta*, Venice, 1504 (O.S. 1503) (RISM 1504[3])
(4) Rome, Biblioteca Apostolica Vaticana, Cappella Giulia, Col. XIII.27
(4) Segovia, Catedral, Codex (Archivo, without signature)
(3) Bologna, Civico Museo Bibliografico Musicale, Ms. Q 18 (*olim* 143)
(3) Seville, Biblioteca Colombina, Cod. 5-I-43 (*olim* Z,135,33)
(2) Florence, Biblioteca Nazionale Centrale, Ms. Fondo Magl. XIX. 178
(2) Berlin, Öffentliche Wissenschaftliche Bibliothek, Ms. 40098 (Glogauer Liederbuch)
(2) Petrucci, *Harmonice musices Odhecaton A*, Venice, 1501 (RISM 1501)
(1) Basel, Universitätsbibliothek, Ms. F. IX. 22 (Kotter Tablature)
(1) Egenolff, *[Lieder zu 3 & 4 Stimmen]*, Frankfurt am Main, *[ca. 1535]* (RISM 1535[14])
(1) Florence, Biblioteca Nazionale Centrale, Ms. Fondo Magl. XIX. 121
(1) Florence, Biblioteca Nazionale Centrale, Ms. Fondo Panciatichiano 27
(1) Paris, Bibliothèque Nationale, Fonds fr. 15123 (*Le Manuscrit Pixérécourt*)
(1) Paris, Bibliothèque Nationale, Réserve Ms. Vm[7]676
(1) Perugia, Biblioteca Comunale, Ms. 431 (*olim* Biblioteca August Cod. G20)
(1) Petrucci, *Canti B. numero cinquanta*, Venice, 1502 (O.S. 1501) (RISM 1502[2])
(1) St. Gall, Stiftsbibliothek, Cod. 461 (Fridolin Sichers Liederbuch)
(1) Trent, Castello del Buonconsiglio, Codex 89
(1) Trent, Castello del Buonconsiglio, Codex 91

A glance at the above list confirms the overwhelming importance of two collections: Rome Casanatense 2856 and Florence Banco Rari 229. Arthur S. Wolff has written a definitive history, complete with inventory and transcriptions, of the Casanatense source;[28] Howard M. Brown is presently editing the Florence manuscript.[29]

From the miniature emblem at the bottom of folio 2' in Casanatense 2856, Wolff concludes that the manuscript originated sometime prior to February, 1490, when Isabella d'Este was married to Gian Francesco Gonzaga.[30] The oval framing contained within the escutcheon plus heraldric information point strongly to ownership by a woman belonging to Duke Ercole's family. Since the framing embraces emblems associated with the Estes and the dukes of Mantua, it seems to follow that the collection must have belonged to Isabella. This also helps to explain the fact that Martini's compositions in Casanatense 2856 far outnumber those by any other composer, for Martini's musical associations with Isabella must have been close in the late 1480's, when the young girl would have been in her early teens. Wolff's conclusions concerning the provenance of the manuscript strongly substantiate observations made in 1965 by Jose M.ª Llorens, and it now seems certain that Casanatense 2856 had indeed been written for Isabella.[31]

Florence Banco Rari 229, according to Anne Bragard, was most probably assembled by Martini and Isaac, a belief supported by the presence, in alternation, of their names for the first nineteen pieces of the collection.[32] Folio 2' of Banco Rari 229 also contains a portrait long thought to represent Martini, although doubt, according to Lewis Lockwood, has been raised by Howard Brown and others.[33] The portrait (if it is that of Martini) is reproduced in Reese.[34]

Together, Casanatense 2856 and Florence 229 contain forty-eight pieces, of which twelve are concordant. Of the other sources containing Martini's secular music, central and northern Italian manuscripts (Verona, Bologna, Florence, Rome, Trent, and Perugia), the Petrucci publications at Venice, and the Spanish manuscripts (Segovia and Seville) account for another thirty-seven pieces, leaving only geographically scattered locations for the remaining twelve instances where his music can be found. Formschneider's *Trium vocum carmina* (1538), which fails to mention the composer by name, seems to have been the last Renaissance collection in which music unquestionably by Martini (*Je remerchi dieu* and *La Martinella*, plus two other possible works) appears.[35] If we may judge from dates usually assigned to all the sources listed immediately above, his fame seems to have died rapidly after the early years of the sixteenth century.

Forty-four secular compositions, of which thirty-one are à 3 and the remainder à 4, may be counted if we include the doubtful works and the one composition for which Martini added a *si placet* Bassus part. One other piece, in Basel F. IX. 22 f. 27'–30, has been excluded on grounds that the work is an organ transcription of Martini's *La Martinella* by another musician and is totally unlike anything known to have been written by Martini.[36] In the secular pieces, French titles predominate; a few have Italian titles. Beyond these, one encounters titles like *Cayphas*, *Der newe pawir schwantcz*, *Groen vint*, and *O intemerata*, and the six pieces without titles in Florence Banco Rari 229.[37] Only two pieces, *Fortuna d'un gran tempo* and *Nenciozza mia*, carry in the sources at least one fully texted part; for the remainder, the scribes and printers merely provided incipits in one or more voices, or sometimes only a title, with or without incipits. This almost total absence of complete texts in the manuscripts and also in contemporary literary sources gives rise to speculations regarding performance practice, a problem discussed by Brawley.[38] Internal evidence in the music itself—phrase syntax frequently truncated by rests, and melodic lines occasionally characterized by awkward leaps, wide ranges, and motivic structures—suggest instrumental performances. These features, frequently found in the secular pieces, can be set against the more obviously vocal music in the Magnificats and Masses, and the differences in musical conception become more readily apparent. Vocally, the secular pieces are not so ingratiating and contain many passages that singers find hard to negotiate.

A passage from the Codex Biblioteca Estense a.H.1,13 lends further weight to the argument that Martini's secular music may have been intended for instrumental performance. On October 15, 1485, Ercole ordered six books from Andrea de le Viese, a calligrapher and gilder, one of which, believed by Wolff to be Casanatense 2856, was described as follows:

> A book of polyphonic music written and notated by Don Alessandro Signorello for the *pifaresca* with an initial page illuminated in an antique style, with the ducal arms, and with antique gold lettering.[39]

Since the collection of instruments at Ferrara was so extensive, most likely the term *pifaresca* used here embraced various kinds of recorders, shawms, and flutes, as well as instruments like bagpipes, trumpets, and trombones; alternatively, it simply may have referred to the players of such instruments. Numerous iconographical references of the time, especially by painters active in northern Italy, show ensembles of instruments whose ranges and general playing characteristics are well suited to Martini's music, evidence further supported by letters, diaries, and other literary sources. If Ercole's book of polyphonic music for the *pifaresca* is the Casanatense 2856, a manuscript which contains more than half of Martini's secular compositions, and if texts for almost all his works in other sources are lacking, instrumental performance seems justified.

Yet we do have, on the other hand, Martini's letter of April 18, 1491 to Isabella wherein he mentions sending her a "cantzon" to sing. If it were one of his own secular pieces, the letter raises at least three additional questions: the identity of the actual piece, the text, if any, accompanying it, and the broader consideration of what kind of music Martini and his contemporaries considered singable. Should additional research bring to light suitable texts which match Martini's titles and neatly adapt to the musical structures found in the secular pieces—many of which roughly divide into two equal parts typical of the literary *rondeau cinquain*—a reassessment in the direction of vocal performances with at least one or more participating voices would follow. But in the most famous collections of poetry of the period (the *Jardin de Plaisance*, the manuscript of the Cardinal of Rohan, among others), poetry matching the titles and incipits of Martini's secular music is lacking. The widespread lack of texts to Martini's music may indicate that the scribes were ignorant of the texts, but that the singers themselves were not, i.e., singers knew the texts from memory and accommodated them to appropriate music. For only five of the forty-four pieces have texts been located which match titles given to Martini's pieces in the sources: *Cela sans plus, Fortuna desperata, Fortuna d'un gran tempo, J'ai pris amours,* and *Nenciozza mia.* If poetic texts were supposed to be so widely known, this is a small number indeed, even if oral transmission of poetic texts by singers was really stronger than we think. Until further evidence justifying vocal performances with texts can be brought forth, instrumental performances seem to be the most appropriate realizations, although a possible combination for performance might include one or more singers vocalizing parts along with instrumentalists.

If we turn to the doubtful pieces, *Cayphas* has been found in only one source, the Segovia manuscript, where two names, "Zohannes Martini" on the recto and "loysete compere" on the verso, appear over the piece. Perhaps the two composers collaborated, since records show that they were together in Milan in the early 1470's.[40] Two compositions by Compère precede *Cayphas* in the manuscript, and the following piece is attributed to that composer. But this sequence does not firmly establish either Compère or Martini as the composer, for the attributions in Segovia are not always trustworthy, and elsewhere in the same manuscript one encounters four consecutive pieces, the first, third, and fourth belonging to one composer, the second to another. Ludwig Finscher fails to mention *Cayphas* in his study of Compère,[41] and internal evidence in the music itself provides no certain attribution to either composer.

Interest, more than doubt, surrounds the piece *Cela sans plus*. If we are to believe the Casanatense manuscript, Martini here added a *si placet* Bassus to a three-part setting of Colinet de Lannoy. Our interest lies in the procedure itself and the unknown reason why it was attempted; the doubt rests on qualitative grounds, for the added part is not exactly a model of suave, smooth melodic writing and falls, I think, below Martini's usual standards. At times the Bassus encumbers the three-part version with contrapuntally awkward passages and complicates the problem of *musica ficta,* especially in one notable place at the final cadence, but his added part does contribute positively by making more complete vertical sonorities and giving clarity to the tonal direction in some parts of the piece.

Der newe pawir schwantcz [a new monkey's tail], found with that title as anonymous in the Glogauer Liederbuch, is identical with *O intemerata* in Segovia, where it is clearly attributed to Martini. In Florence Banco Rari 229, the same composition carries no title or attribution, an inexplicable omission if Martini himself had figured prominently in assembling the complete collection. John Brawley considers this same piece a motet.[42] Its inclusion in the secular collection Banco Rari 229 and the title given in Glogauer may confirm the piece as secular, and on these grounds it is included in this edition.

Of ten versions of *Des biens d'amours* à 3 and à 4, only two sources attribute the composition to Martini. Whereas Banco Rari 229 names Martini, Florence Panciatichiano 27 names Yzach (=Isaac). A third source, Florence 178, shows "Jos" and "Martin" at the tops of folios 44'–45 respectively. I read this as Johannes Martini, although Bianca Becherini erroneously, I think, claims Josquin as the composer.[43] The scribe of Florence 178 characteristically wrote "Josqn," "Josquin," or "Josquin Despres" for compositions by Josquin and in instances where the full name of any composer was used, wrote given names and surnames on facing pages, as for example, Johannes Martini, Josquin Despres, Enricus Yzac, Loyset Compère, etc. The evidence in the manuscript, therefore, clearly points to Martini as the composer of *Des biens d'amours*. The remaining eight sources give no attributions. Although some doubt to Martini's claim may be cast by the Panciatichi ascription to Isaac, the unusual alternation of attributions to Martini and Isaac in the opening folios of Banco Rari 229 argues convincingly for Martini, as a glance at the inventory would confirm. Another question surrounds the four-part version of the piece *Des biens d'amours* found in Bologna Q 18. That Martini added the altus to his own three-part composition seems unlikely, for the fourth part in Bologna Q 18 obscures the beauty of the three-part version and is even far less artistic than Martini's *si placet* Bassus to Lannoy's *Cela sans plus.* The four-part version has been included here as a doubtful work.

The *J'ay pris amours* setting in Segovia is identical, except for minor variants, to that in *Odhecaton A*, where it is assigned to Busnois. The general reliability of the Petrucci publication weighs heavily in favor of Busnois, but on stylistic grounds both composers could lay substantial claims to authorship. In fact, the case for Martini rests on stronger musical grounds, in this editor's opinion, than that for Busnois. For the moment, however, any definite attribution must remain an open issue.

Malheur me bat, another doubtful piece, is found in nine sources:

Florence Banco Rari 229, f. 10'–11 (Janes Mātini)
Rome Cappella Giulia XIII.27, f. 72'–73 (Io. Martini)
Petrucci, *Odhecaton A.,* f. 68'–69 (Ockenghem)
St. Gall 461, f. 52–53 (Ockenghem)
Rome Casanatense 2856, f. 57'–59 (Malcort)

Bologna Q 16, f. 22'–23 (Anon.)
Bologna Q 18, f. 73'–74 (Anon.)
Egenolff, *Lieder* (RISM 1535[4]), No. 58 (Anon.)
Formschneider, *Trium vocum carmina* (RISM 1538[9]), No. 91 (Anon.)

Three composers, Martini, Ockeghem, and Malcort are thus named in five sources where attributions are given. The early sixteenth-century theorist, Pietro Aron, named Ockeghem as the composer.[44] Aron's treatise and St. Gall 461 probably depended upon *Odhecaton A* for assignation to Ockeghem, but all these sources postdate Banco Rari 229, where evidence in the opening folios of the manuscript strongly supports an attribution to Martini. Malcort's claim has not found support among modern scholars, most of whom have favored Ockeghem, but Wolff maintains that Malcort's name cannot be entirely discounted in view of the high reliability of attributions found in Casanatense 2856.[45] Brawley, however, cogently reasons on behalf of Martini, citing bibliographical factors which, he believes, tend to deny authorship to Ockeghem and rather positively point to Martini as the probable composer of *Malheur me bat*.[46]

One piece included in this edition is nowhere attributed to Martini, nor to any other composer. *Sol fa mi fa sol* (No. 43 in this edition) is found as a *Martinella* in three sources (Casanatense 2856, Florence Banco Rari 229, and Rome Cappella Giulia XIII.27), as *Seruitur* in Paris Vm[7]676, and titleless in Formschneider (No. 35). The piece may be by Martini; it bears an obvious relationship to Martini's more famous *Martinella*, whose head motive it employs, but the evidence is inconclusive. Rhythmic, melodic, and contrapuntal features fall within Martini's compositional techniques, leading Wolff to observe that Martini had probably composed "another arrangement . . . bearing the stamp of his own celebrated tune."[47]

Extended discussions of stylistic features in Martini's secular music are few, although numerous scholars have made shorter contributions. Three references can be cited. The first, a master's thesis by Charlotte Greenspan, contains many useful observations.[48] John Brawley systematically touches every aspect of Martini's secular style, always with historical insight and balanced judgment.[49] Brawley's study is the most complete to date. Theodore Karp's article, critical and informative, clearly calls for more detailed studies relating to style characteristics he touches upon.[50] Taken together, these studies provide an introductory survey and analysis of phrase syntax, rhythmic patterns, form, and other aspects of Martini's secular music. But they also raise, as prolegomena to future investigations, intriguing questions, particular as well as general, chronological as well as stylistic. Much information may be lost forever, but some of the questions may eventually be answered with time and patient scholarship.

EDITORIAL PROCEDURES

Editorial procedures were formulated once certain basic decisions had been made. First, and foremost, the editor wanted to present Martini, as composer, in the best possible light. In the case of the unica, a single transcription had to suffice; of necessity, each transcription had to be literally rendered. Where two or more versions of the same piece existed, I attempted to choose the most musical reading and to transcribe it as faithfully as I did the unica. Thus, every one of the forty-four pieces actually stands as a transcription from some single source. Only in those instances in which obvious scribal errors were encountered do the transcriptions differ from the original; these relatively few variants have been listed under Critical Notes. Against each final version I noted all variants from other concordant pieces. The entire method at least ensures that every piece printed here preserves in transcription the integrity of its source and that it serves as a model against which other sources can readily be compared.

All the transcription sources appear in conventional white notation. Note values have been reduced by half, the breve (𝄎) being rendered as a whole-note. Original time signatures, given in the incipits, are, with six exceptions, *in tempus imperfectum diminutum* (₵). Three of the exceptions are in *tempus imperfectum, proportio dupla* (C). Three others, *Fortuna d'un gran tempo*, *Que je fasoye*, and *Sans siens du mal*, carry ₵3 signatures. In those duple meter pieces where Martini introduces brief passages in triple meter, the manuscripts and prints simply employ the symbol 3.

Five pieces involved text underlay, but in only one instance, *Fortuna d'un gran tempo*, did the text come directly from the transcribed source. For the other four pieces, texts were derived; all textual additions have been set within brackets to distinguish them from an original incipit (or lack of it) in the transcription source.

Modern G and F clefs replace the older C clefs and the less frequent "baritone" clef. For the thirteen four-part pieces, Martini used nine different combinations of clefs. For the thirty-one three-part pieces, he shows preference for MS, T, B (10) and S, T, B (8) combinations. Incipits in this edition show the original clef, the first note, and key signature. Also given is the ambitus of each part, a feature useful to performers. Original ligatures have been indicated by horizontal brackets (⌐¬), coloration by broken brackets (⌐ ¬), embracing the passages in question. All accidentals

xiv

appearing in the original sources have been retained with one exception: the flat sign appearing before "f" in the superius of measure 45 of *Sol la si do si*. Editorial accidentals are placed above notes where *musica ficta* practices may apply; a few cautionary accidentals are also placed above notes and enclosed in parentheses, usually as reminders of original inflections. Conventions in the application of *musica ficta* solve some, but not all, of the vexing problems that arise, and thus the editorial suggestions may satisfy some tastes and not others.

ABBREVIATIONS, TRANSCRIPTION SOURCES, CONCORDANCES, AND CRITICAL NOTES

Sources of the transcriptions, concordances, modern printed editions, variants, critical notes, and a table of abbreviations are given below. Each numbered piece has been given a title, usually modernized in spelling. The number of voices is given in parentheses. The word "Transcription" has been reserved for the single source from which the printed transcription in this edition is taken. Under each listed source the composer's name and the incipit for each voice are set forth; all orthographical peculiarities have been retained. Completeness of text in each voice is indicated as follows:

(t) = full text
(i) = incipit only
(−) = no text or incipit

Where modern printed editions exist, these are referred to under that heading. No attempt was made to list transcriptions found in dissertations by John Brawley and Arthur S. Wolff (see fn. 9).

Sources listed under "Transcription" and "Concordance(s)" have been given in an abbreviated form under "Variants" according to the table below. After much deliberation, it was finally decided to register all variants by measure numbers according to the printed transcriptions. This method has the disadvantage of not permitting quick appraisals of how closely sources match, but it has one decidedly practical value: it allows players who perform this music to quickly compare given passages for musical effectiveness. Where the differences encountered are extensive, for example, the Cappella Giulia version of *Malheur me bat*, fully notated passages have been provided.

A few critical and explanatory notes of interest have been included under sections labelled Concordances, Modern Editions, or Variants.

Abbreviations

Manuscripts:

Basel	Basel, Universitätsbibliothek, Ms. F. IX. 22 (Kotter Tablature) (1545)
Casa	Rome, Biblioteca Casanatense, Ms. 2856 (*ca.*1485)
Flo 27	Florence, Biblioteca Nazionale Centrale, Ms. Fondo Panciatichiano 27 (*ca.*1500)
Flo 121	Florence, Biblioteca Nazionale Centrale, Ms. Fondo Magl. XIX. 121 (*ca.*1500)
Flo 178	Florence, Biblioteca Nazionale Centrale, Ms. Fondo Magl. XIX. 178 (early 16th c.)
Flo 229	Florence, Biblioteca Nazionale Centrale, Ms. Banco Rari 229 (*olim* Magl. XIX. 59) (*ca.*1500)
G XIII.27	Rome, Biblioteca Apostolica Vaticana, Cappella Giulia, Col. XIII.27 (16th c.)
Glogauer	Berlin, Öffentliche Wissenschaftliche Bibliothek, Ms. 40098 (Glogauer Liederbuch) (*ca.*1477–88)
Paris	Paris, Bibliothèque Nationale, Fonds fr. 15123 (*Le Manuscrit Pixérécourt*) (*ca.*1500)
Paris 676	Paris, Bibliothèque Nationale, Réserve Ms. Vm^{7}676 (dated 1502)
Perugia	Perugia, Biblioteca Comunale, Ms. 431 (*olim* Biblioteca August Cod. G20) (*ca.*1500)
Q 16	Bologna, Civico Museo Bibliografico Musicale, Ms. Q 16 (*olim* 109) (*ca.*1490)
Q 18	Bologna, Civico Museo Bibliografico Musicale, Ms. Q 18 (*olim* 143) (*ca.*1500–20)
Segovia	Segovia, Catedral, Codex (Archivo, without signature) (*ca.*1500)
Seville	Seville, Biblioteca Colombina, Cod. 5-I-43 (*olim* Z,135,33) (late 15th c.)
St. Gall	St. Gall, Stiftsbibliothek, Cod. 461 (Fridolin Sichers Liederbuch) (dated 1545)
Trent 89	Trent, Castello del Buonconsiglio, Codex 89 (15th c.)
Trent 91	Trent, Castello del Buonconsiglio, Codex 91 (15th c.)
Verona	Verona, Biblioteca Capitolare, Cod. Mus. 757 (early 16th c.)

Early printed books:

Canti B — *Canti B. numero cinquanta*, Venice, O. Petrucci, 1502 (O.S. 1501) (RISM 1502[2])

Canti C — *Canti C. numero cento cinquanta*, Venice, O. Petrucci, 1504 (O.S. 1503) (RISM 1504[3])

Egenolff — [Lieder zu 3 & 4 Stimmen], Frankfurt am Main, Christian Egenolff, [*ca.* 1535] (RISM 1535[14])

Form — *Trium vocum carmina a diversis musicis composita*, Nuremberg, H. Formschneider, 1538 (RISM 1538[9])

Odhecaton A — *Harmonice musices Odhecaton A*, Venice, Ottaviano Petrucci, 1501 (RISM 1501)

Transcription Sources, Concordances, and Critical Notes

1. *Biaulx parle tousjours* (à 3)

TRANSCRIPTION (unicum)—Rome Casanatense 2856, f. 129'–130', "Jo. martini": "Biaulx parle tosjours" (i); "Biaulx pâle" (i); "Biaulx parle" (i).

VARIANT—Mm. 32–34, A, Casa reads nine beats of rests.

2. *Cayphas* (à 3)

TRANCRIPTION (unicum)—Segovia, f. 185, "loysete compere Zohañes Martini": "(C)ayphas" (i); "Cayphas" (i); "Cayphas" (i).

VARIANTS—M. 28, B, beat 4 half-note in Segovia. M. 44, T, third note f in Segovia.

3. *Cela sans plus* (à 4)

TRANSCRIPTION—Rome Casanatense 2856, f. 153'–154, "Colinet de Lanoy": "Se la sans plus" (i); (i); (i); (–). Bassus reads "si placet" by "Jo. Martini." Incipits in Casa read "Se," not "Ce-."

CONCORDANCE—Petrucci, Canti B, f. 19'–20, Anon. (Index: "Lanuoy"): "Cela sans plus" (i); (–); (i); (–).

MODERN EDITIONS—(a) Jacob Obrecht, *Werken*, ed. Johannes Wolf, *Wereldlijke Werken*, p. 83. (b) Petrucci, *Canti B*, ed. Helen Hewitt, p. 137. (This edition provides the text.)

VARIANTS—Bassus part by Martini is identical in Casanatense 2856 and Canti B. For variants in other voices, consult Helen Hewitt's edition of Canti B.

4. *De la bonne chiere* (à 3)

TRANSCRIPTION (unicum)—Rome Casanatense 2856, f. 132'–133, "Jo. Martini": "De la bonne chiere" (i); (i); (i).

MODERN EDITION—Theodore Karp, "The Secular Works of Johannes Martini" in *Aspects of Medieval and Renaissance Music*, p. 469.

5. *[Der newe pawir schwantcz]* (à 3)

TRANSCRIPTION—Florence Banco Rari 229, f. 129'–130, Anon.: (–); (–); (–).

CONCORDANCES—(a) Glogauer Liederbuch, No. 257, Anon.: "Der newe pawir schwantcz" (i); (i); (i). (b) Segovia, f. 172', "Johanes Martini": "O intemerata" (i); (i); (i).

VARIANTS—M. 3, C, two half-notes in Glogauer and Segovia. M. 4, C, two half-notes in Segovia. M. 9, C and T, rhythm half, quarter, quarter in Glogauer. M. 10, C, two half-notes in Glogauer; T, two half-notes in Glogauer and Segovia. M. 12, CT, whole-note in Segovia. M. 14, CT, b is flatted in Glogauer. M. 15, CT, dotted-half (g), quarter (f) in Glogauer, whole-note (g) in Segovia. M. 17, C, beats 1–2, half-note in Segovia. M. 18, C, beats 1–2, quarter-note (c"), eighth-note (b'), eighth-note (a') in Glogauer. M. 19, C, two half-notes in Segovia; CT, first note c in Segovia, first note half-rest in Glogauer. M. 20, CT, first note a in Glogauer and Segovia. M. 21, CT, rhythm half, quarter, quarter in Glogauer. M. 27, C, first two notes dotted-quarter and eighth in Segovia, CT, half note d, half-note f in Glogauer and Segovia. M. 29, C and CT, whole-notes in Segovia. M. 33, CT, second note c in Glogauer, three half-notes (e, c, e) in Segovia. M. 35, CT, half-note, half-rest, half-note in Glogauer. M. 42, CT, note 1, no flat in Glogauer or Segovia. M. 43, CT, first note whole-note in Segovia. M. 45, CT, three half-notes (g, e, d) in Segovia. M. 48, T, whole-note, half-note in Segovia. M. 52, CT, first two notes b, a in Segovia and Glogauer; last note c in Segovia.

6. *Des biens d'amours* (Version A—à 3)

TRANSCRIPTION—Rome Casanatense 2856, f. 5'–6, Anon.: "Des biens damours" (i); (i); (i).

CONCORDANCES—(a) Bologna Q 16, f. 9'–10 (Arabic foliation), Anon.: "Des biens" (i); (i); (i). (b) Bologna Q 18, f. 64'–65, Anon.: "(d)es biens damors" (i); (–); (–); (–); (see No. 7, Version B). (c) Florence Pan 27, f. 49'–50, "Yzach": "Les bien amore" (i); (–); (–). (d) Florence 121, f. 29'–30, Anon.: (–); (–); (–). (e) Florence 178, f. 44'–45, "Jõs Martin": "La re" (i); (–); (–). (f) Florence 229, f. 18'–19, "Jannes Martini": "(D)es biens" (i); (–); (–). (g) Formschneider, No. 77, Anon.: (–); (–); (–). (h) Perugia 431, f. 87'–88, Anon.: "De biens damoris" (i); (i); (–). (i) Rome G XIII.27, f. 44'–45, Anon.: "De biens" (i); (–); (–).

VARIANTS—First half measure is not in Flo 121, Flo 178, Flo 229, G XIII.27, and Form. Flat signature (in Bassus) is not in Flo 178, G XIII.27, and Form; it appears on first staff only of Flo 229. Mm. 1–2, T, only one and one-half measure rest in Perugia. M. 4, B, two half-notes in Flo 121, Flo 178, Flo 229, and G XIII.27.

M. 5, B, half-note (A), half-note (a) in Flo 27. M. 6, B, first note f in Flo 27. M. 8, A, half-note (c') in last half measure in Q 16. M. 9, B, notated b-flat in Flo 27 and Form. M. 10, A, notated b-flat in Form. M. 11, T, notated b-flat in Form. Mm. 17–19, T, dotted-quarter (e), eighth (f), quarter (g), quarter (a) tied over barline to quarter (a), quarter (g), quarter (a), quarter (c') tied over barline to quarter (c'), eighth (b) eighth (a), dotted-quarter (g), eighth (f) in Flo 27; B, quarter (A), half (c), eighth (B), eighth (A), barline, half (d), quarter (A), quarter (a) tied over barline to quarter (a), eighth (g), eighth (f), half (e) in Flo 27. M. 17, A, whole-note in Flo 27. M. 18, A, whole-note in Perugia. Mm. 18-19, A, tied whole-notes in Form; half-rest, half-note tied to half-note, half-note in Flo 27. M. 18, T, first note is f in Flo 178. M. 19, A, two half-notes in Flo 121, Flo 229, Q 16, Flo 178, G XIII.27, and Perugia. Mm. 20–21, B, half-note B-flat (scribal error?) in Flo 178. M. 21, B, quarter-rest at beginning of measure in Q 16. M. 22, B, last note B-flat in Flo 178 (scribal error?). M. 23, A, dotted-eighth (d'), sixteenth (e') at beginning of measure in Q 16; third note c'' in Form. Mm. 23–38 are compressed in Flo 27 as follows:

M. 24, A, notated b-flat in Form. M. 29, A, notated b-flat in Form. M. 31, T, notated b-flat in Form; rhythm quarter, half, eighth, eighth in Q 16, Flo 178, Flo 229, G XIII.27. Mm.33–35, A, quarter (d'), quarter (f'), quarter (g'), quarter (f'), barline, half (f'), quarter (g'), quarter (a') tied over barline to eighth (a'), eighth (g'), quarter (f'), quarter (e') in Q 16; T, quarter (d), quarter (d'), quarter (b), quarter (a), barline, half (d'), quarter (e'), quarter (f') tied over barline to eighth (f'), eighth (e'), quarter (d'), quarter (c') in Q 16. M. 34, B, notated b-flat in Flo 178 and Flo 229; last two notes dotted-quarter and eighth in Q 16. M. 35, B, dotted-half in Flo 178, Flo 229, and G XIII. 27. M. 37, A, two half-notes in Q 16; T, beats 1–3, quarter-rest, half-note in Flo 121, Flo 178, Flo 229, G XIII.27, Form, Perugia 431. Mm. 38–39, A, tie over barline in Perugia. M. 38, T, notated b-flat in Form. M. 39, A, whole-note in Form. Mm. 39–40, A, half-note, half-note tied over barline to half-note, half-note in Flo 121. M. 39, B, notated b-flat in Form. Mm. 39–40, B, notes tied over barline in Form. M. 40, B, two half-notes, m. 41, B, no tie, m. 42, B, dotted-half (A), quarter (c), m. 43, B, quarter (B), quarter (d), quarter (c), quarter (G) in Perugia. Mm. 40–42, B, half, half, half, half, whole (no tie) in G XIII.27; half, half, half, half, half, half, (no tie) in Flo 121, Flo 178, Flo 229, Q 16, M.41, A, two half-notes in Flo 229, G XIII.27, Q 16. Mm. 41–42, A, tied whole-notes in Flo 178, Form; half, half, whole in Perugia. M. 41, T, beats 1–3, dotted-quarter (a), sixteenth (g), sixteenth (f), quarter (e) in Q 16. Mm. 41–42, T, half (a), quarter (f), quarter (e), no tie, half (a), eighth (g), eighth (f), quarter (e) in Perugia. M. 44, A, beats 3–4, half-note (c') in Flo 121, Flo 229 G XIII.27. Mm. 45–47, B, half (a), quarter (b), quarter (a) tied over barline to quarter (a), eighth (g), eighth (f), half (e), barline, quarter (f) in Flo 27. M. 48, A, eighth (c''), eighth (d''), eighth (c''), sixteenth (b'), sixteenth (a'), dotted-quarter (g'), eighth (F') in Q 16; beats 3–4, half-note (g') in Flo 178, Flo 229, G XIII.27. M. 49, T, beats 3–4, dotted-quarter (g), eighth (f) in Q 16, Perugia, and Form. M. 53, A, quarter (a'), dotted-quarter (f'), eighth (g'), eighth (f'), sixteenth (e'), sixteenth (d') in Q 16.

7. *Des biens d'amours* (Version B—à 4)
   TRANSCRIPTION—Bologna Q18, f. 64'–65, Anon.: "(D)es biens damors" (i); (–); (–); (–).
   CONCORDANCES—See No. 6, "Des biens d'amours" (Version A), the three-part setting. In Q 18, the added voice is the Altus, an addition which requires a modification of *musica ficta* suggestions.

Dieu damors (See No. 25.)

8. *Fault il que heur soye* (à 4)
   TRANSCRIPTION (unicum)—Petrucci, *Canti C*, f. 72'–74, "Jo. martini": "Fault il q̃ heur soy" (i); "Fault il" (i); "Fault il" (i).
   VARIANTS—M. 45, CB-I, first note incorrectly f in Canti C. M. 79, CB-I, g, e, f in Canti C; last note f in error?

9. *Fortuna desperata* (à 4)

TRANSCRIPTION (unicum)—Rome Casanatense 2856, f. 147′–149, "Jo martini": "Fortuna disperata" (i); (i); (i); "fortuna" (i). The added text in the cantus can be found in Fausto Torrefranco, *Il segreto del quattrocento* (after Perugia 431 and Paris Vm⁷676. The lower three voices are obviously not well suited to a vocal text.

10. *Fortuna d'un gran tempo* (à 4)

TRANSCRIPTION (unicum)—Florence Banco Rari 229, f. 156′–158, "Jannes Martini": "Fortuna dun grã tempo" (t), "fortuna" (i); "fortuna dun gran tẽpo" (t); "fortuna" (i). No attempt has been made to underlay a text in the contratenor and contrabassus parts.

11. *Fuga ad quatuor* (à 4)

TRANSCRIPTION (unicum)—Rome Casanatense 2856, f. 47, "Jo Martini": "Fuga ad quatuor" (i); (−); (−); (−).

MODERN EDITION—J. A. L. de la Fage, *Essais de diphtherographie musicale*, II, p. 32.

12. *Fuge la morie* (à 3)

TRANSCRIPTION—Rome Casanatense 2856, f. 102′–104, "Jo Martini": "Fuge la morie" (i); (i); (i).

CONCORDANCES—(a) Florence Banco Rari 229, f. 148′–149, Anon.: (−); (−); (−). (b) Segovia, f. 189′, "Johannes Martini": "Groen vint" (i); (i); (i).

VARIANTS—M. 13, C, first note dotted-half in Segovia. M. 23, T, rhythm half, dotted-quarter, sixteenth, sixteenth in Flo 229. M. 39, C, beats 3–4, dotted-quarter (c′), eighth (b) in Segovia and Flo 229. M. 51, C, second note is d′ in Segovia and Flo 229.

(G)arde(s) vous donc (See No. 37.)

Groen vint (See No 12.)

13. *Helas coment* (Version A—à 3)

TRANSCRIPTION—Florence Banco Rari 229, f. 101′–102, "Jannes Martini": "Helas coment" (i); (i); (i).

CONCORDANCE—Bologna Q 16, f. 57′–58, Anon.: "Hellas comêt anes" (i); "Hellas" (i); "Hellas coment" (i).

VARIANTS—The Florence and Bologna versions differ rather extensively; a separate version is given for each. Compare No. 13 and No. 14.

14. *Hellas coment anes* (Version B—à 3)

TRANSCRIPTION—Bologna Q 16, f. 57′–58, (Arabic foliation), Anon.: "Hellas comet anes" (i); "Hellas" (i); "Hellas coment" (i).

CONCORDANCE—See No. 13, "Helas coment."

15. *Il est tel* (à 3)

TRANSCRIPTION—Rome Casanatense 2856, f. 76′–78, "Jo martini": "Il est tel" (i); (i); (i).

CONCORDANCE—Florence Banco Rari 229, f. 290′, "Jannes Martini": (i); (i); (missing). Only Cantus and a part of the Tenor are preserved; Bassus is missing.

VARIANTS—M. 20, C, beat 1, eighth (d′), eighth (c′) in Flo 229. M. 21, C and T, no ties over barline in Flo 229. M. 24, T, last note a in Flo 229. M. 32, C, dotted-quarter (g′), eighth (f′), quarter (g′), quarter (a′) tied to a′ in m. 33 in Flo 229. M. 33, T, first beat is quarter-note a in Flo 229.

16. *[Il est tousjours]* (à 3)

TRANSCRIPTION—Florence Banco Rari 229, f. 16′–17, "Jo martini": (−); (−); (−).

CONCORDANCE—Rome Casanatense 2856, f. 112′–113, "Jo. Martini": "Il est tousjours" (i); (−); (i).

VARIANTS—Casa 2856 is incomplete. Superius lacks measure 36 to end; Tenor is missing measures 1–35; and Contratenor skips from measure 17 (beat 4) to measure 57 (beat 3). M. 9, CT, half (d′), half (c′) in Flo 229 (error?). M. 21, C, second note b′ in Flo 229 (error?). M. 33, C, half (a′), quarter (a′), quarter (b′) in Casa 2856. M. 52, C, first note g′ in Flo 229 (error?).

17. *J'ay pris amours* (Version A—à 4)

TRANSCRIPTION (unicum)—Florence Banco Rari 229, f. 189′–190, "Jannes Martini": "(J)ay pris amours" (i); (i); (−); "Canon I. pre-sequar" (−).

CONCORDANCES—Consult Helen Hewitt's edition of *Odhecaton A*, pp. 139–141 and p. 131 for other settings. The tenor parts of Version A and B in this edition stand with inverted intervals to each other, the Cantus and Tenor parts of Version A being identical to those in the three-part Dijon 517 piece, considered the most antique setting.

18. *J'ay pris amours* (Version B—à 4)

TRANSCRIPTION—Segovia, f. 110′, "Johannes martini": "(J)ay prys amours" (i); (i); (i); (i). "Canon: Antifrasis tenorizat / ypsodum epiton pluzat." The text underlaid in this edition is from f. 71′ of *Le Jardin de plaisance*, facsimile edition by Eugénie Droz and Arthur Piaget (Paris, 1910).

CONCORDANCE—Petrucci, *Odhecaton A*, f. 44′–50, "Busnoys": "Jay pris amours tout au rebours" (i); "Jay pris amours" (i); (i); (i).

MODERN EDITIONS—Obrecht, *Wereldlijke Werken*, p. 96. Petrucci, *Odhecaton A*, edited by Helen Hewitt, p. 305.

VARIANTS—Petrucci shows one-flat signature throughout all parts. M. 1, A, rest missing in Segovia. M. 4, T-I, whole-note (a) in Petrucci. M. 9, A, last beat eighth (f′), eighth (e′) in Odhecaton A. M. 13, A, first beat eighth (e′), eighth (d′) in Odhecaton A. M. 14, T-I, tie in Odhecaton A, T-II, rhythm quarter, half, eighth, eighth in Odhecaton A. M. 16, T-II, half-rest, dotted-quarter (g), eighth (a) in Odhecaton A. M. 31, A, dotted-half (f′), eighth (e′), eighth (d′) in Odhecaton

A; B, beats 1–3, quarter (d), half (f), in Odhecaton A. M. 32, T-I, half-note, half-rest in Odhecaton A. M. 37, B, half (d), quarter (d), quarter (g) in Odhecaton A. M. 41, T-I, last beat eighth (g), eighth (a) in Odhecaton A. M. 43, T-II, half (f'), half (c') in Odhecaton A. M. 45, A, second beat eighth (g'), eighth (f') in Odhecaton A; B, second beat eighth (e), eighth (d) in Odhecaton A. M. 55, A, quarter (e'), quarter (f'), half (g') in Odhecaton A. Mm. 56–57, T-II, dotted-quarter (d'), eighth (c'), quarter (a), quarter (a) tied over barline to quarter (a), quarter (f), half (e) in Odhecaton A.

19. *Je remerchi dieu* (à 3)
TRANSCRIPTION—Rome Casanatense 2856, f. 120'–121, "Jo. martini": "Ie remerchi dieu" (i); (i); (−).
CONCORDANCES—(a) Florence Banco Rari 229, f. 4'–5, "Jannes matini": "Se mai il cielo e fati fur benigni" (i); (−); "Se mai il cielo" (i). (b) Florence 178, f. 65'–66, "Johañes Martini": "Se mai il cielo e fati fur benigni" (i); (−); (−). (c) Verona 757, f. 11'–12, Anon.: (−); (−); (−). (d) Formschneider, No. 21, Anon.: (−); (−); (−).
VARIANTS—M. 13, C, quarter (b'), eighth (a'), eighth (g'), dotted-quarter (f'), eighth (e') in Flo 178 and Flo 229; quarter (b'), eighth (a'), eighth (g'), dotted-quarter (g'), eighth (f') in Verona; quarter (b'), eighth (a'), eighth (g'), dotted-quarter (f'), sixteenth (e'), sixteenth (f') in Form. M. 16, T, quarter (e'), dotted-quarter (d'), eighth (c'), quarter (c') in Form. M. 17, C, first note d' in Flo 178. M. 21, C, last beat eighth (b'), eighth (a') in Form. M. 24, C, first beat eighth (a'), eighth (g') in Flo 178, Flo 229, Verona, Form. M. 26, C, half-note g' tied to g' in m. 25 in Form. M. 29, B, notated b-flat in Flo 178, Flo 229, and Verona. Mm. 31–32, B, quarter-note (a) on last beat of m. 31 tied to quarter-note (a) on first beat of m. 32 in Flo 178, Flo 229, Verona, and Form. M. 35, C, quarter-note (g') on first beat in Verona. M. 42, C, quarter-note (d'') on first beat in Form. Mm. 43–44, T, beats 3 and 4 of measure 43 and the entire measure 44 are omitted in Flo 178.

20. *J'espoir mieulx* (à 3)
TRANSCRIPTION—Rome Casanatense 2856, f. 88'–90, "Jo. martini": "Iespoir mieulx" (i); "Iespoir" (i); "Iespoir" (i).
CONCORDANCE—Florence Banco Rari 229, f. 14'–15, "Janes martini": (−); (−); (−).
VARIANTS—None, except for ligatures and minor coloration.

21. *La fleur de biaulte* (à 4)
TRANSCRIPTION (unicum)—Petrucci, Canti C, f. 69'–70, "Jo. martini": "La fleur de biaulte" (i); "La fleur" (i); "La fleur" (i); "La fleur" (i).
VARIANT—M. 33, CT, whole-note (f'), half-note (g') in Petrucci (error?).

22. *La Martinella* (à 3)
TRANSCRIPTION—Rome Casanatense 2856, f. 55'–57, "Jo martini": "La martinellé" (i); (i); (i).
CONCORDANCES—(a) Basel F. IX.22, f. 27'–30, "Isacio compositori" (in tablature). (b) Bologna, Q 16, f. 93'–94, Anon.: "La martinella" (i); (i); (i). (c) Formschneider, No. 36, Anon.: (−); "La martinella" (i); (−). (d) Florence Banco Rari 229, f. 12'–13, "Jañes Martini": "Martinella" (i); (−); (i). (e) Glogauer Liederbuch, No. 268, Anon.: (−); (−); (−). (f) Paris 15123, f. 145'–147, Anon.: "La martinella" (i); (i); (i). (g) Rome Giulia XIII.27, f. 36'–38, "Johannes Martini": "Martinella" (i); (−); (−). (h) Seville 5-I-43, f. 14', Anon.: "(L)amartinella" (i); (−); (−); . (i) Trent 89, f. 389'–390, "Jañes Martini": (−); (−); (−); (DTOe No. 752). (j) Trent 91, f. 257'–258, Anon.: "La martinella" (i); (−); (−); (DTOe No. 1363). (k) Verona 757, f. 17'–18, Anon.: (−); (−); (−).
MODERN EDITIONS—(a) DTOe, VII, p. 223. Transcription of Trent 89, f. 389'–390, but not entirely reliable. (b) *Das Glogauer Liederbuch*, ed. Heribert Ringmann, in *Das Erbe deutscher Musik*, IV, p. 62. (c) *Alte Meister aus der Frühzeit des Orgelspiels*, ed. Arnold Schering, p. 34. An arrangement for keyboard. (d) Brawley, John G. Jr., *The Magnificats, Hymns, Motets, and Secular Compositions of Johannes Martini*, unpublished Ph.D. dissertation, Yale University, 1968, II, p. 196. Transcription of the Basel tablature.
VARIANTS—M. 3, C, dotted-half (b'), eighth (a'), eighth (g') in Q 16. M. 4, C, no tie in G XIII.27. M. 6, T, no tie in G XIII.27. M. 7, C, second beat eighth (a'), eighth (g') in Verona; T, second beat eighth (f), eighth (e) in Verona. M. 8, C, third beat eighth (b'), eighth (c'') in Verona; T, third beat eighth (g), eighth (a) in Verona. M. 9, C, second beat eighth (c''), eighth (b') in Verona, third beat eighth (a'), eighth (b') in Glogauer, third beat quarter (b') in Form; T, second beat eighth (a), eighth (g) in Verona. Mm. 10–11, C, eighth (c''), eighth (b'), eighth (a'), eighth (g'), quarter (f'), quarter (b') tied over barline to eighth (b'), eighth (a'), half (g'), quarter (f') in Seville. M. 11, C, first beat tied eighth-note (b'), eighth-note (a') in Form, Flo 229, Trent 89; T, first beat quarter-note (d') in Q 16, Paris, Trent 91, and Verona. M. 12, C, half-note, half-rest in Verona. M. 15, T, notated e'-flat in Form and Verona. M. 16, B, quarter (g), quarter (f), dotted-quarter (e), eighth (d) in Glogauer. M. 18, B, second beat quarter-note (B) in Q 16, Glogauer. M. 19, B, beats 3–4, half-note (d) in Form, Flo 229, and Trent 89. M. 20, C, half (d'), quarter-rest, quarter (a') in Q 16. M. 21, B, quarter (g), eighth (f), eighth (e), quarter (d), quarter (f) in Form, Flo 229, Trent 89. M. 24, B, no tie in Q 16, Paris, Verona; quarter (e), eighth (d), eighth (c) in Form, Flo 229, Trent 89; notated e-flat in Q 16, Form, Flo 229, G

XIII.27, Trent 89, Trent 91, and Verona. M. 25, T, beats 1–3, dotted-half in G XIII.27, Q 16, Glogauer, and Verona; second beat eighth (a), eighth (g) in Form, Flo 229, and Trent 89. M. 26, T, first beat quarter-note (a) in Paris, Trent 91, Q 16, Glogauer, and Verona. M. 27, C, first two beats quarter (b'), eighth (a'), eighth (g') in Form, Flo 229, Trent 89; first three beats dotted-half in Q 16, G XIII.27, Seville, Verona; B, rhythm quarter-note, quarter-rest, quarter-note, quarter-note in Form, Flo 229, and Trent 89. M. 28, C, first beat quarter-note (a') in Glogauer. Mm. 29–40, B, read as follows in Form, Flo 229, and Trent 89:

M. 30, T, rhythm quarter, half, eighth, eighth in Form, Flo 229, Trent 89, Verona; B, notated e-flat in Q 16, Trent 91, and Verona. M. 32, C, eighth (d'), eighth (e'), eighth (f'), eighth (g'), quarter (a'), tied quarter (b') in Q 16. M. 33, T, notated e'-flat in Form, Flo 229, Glogauer. M. 37, C, first beat quarter (d'), no tie, in Glogauer, tied quarter (a') in Q 16, and tied eighth (a'), eighth (d') in Form, Flo 229, and Trent 89; T, half (b), half (a) in Form, Flo 229, Trent 89; B, first note g in Q 16, Glogauer. M. 38, C, no tie in G XIII.27, last note e' (no tie) in Form. M. 39, C, last note quarter (g) in Glogauer, second two beats dotted-quarter, eighth in Flo 229, Trent 89; B, no notated e-flat in Paris. Mm. 40–41, T, no tie in Flo 229, Trent 89; B, tie in Q 16, Form. M. 42, B, second beat eighth (c), eighth (B) in Form, Flo 229, Trent 89. M. 43, B, quarter (A), quarter (g), quarter (f), quarter (d) (tied to d in m. 44) in Trent 89 (A should be G?). M. 44, B, first beat eighth (e), eighth (d) in G XIII.27, Paris. M. 46, B, first beat tied eighth (f), eighth (d) in Glogauer. Mm. 51–52, B, dotted-quarter (g), eighth (a), quarter (b), quarter (a) tied over barline to quarter (a), eighth (g), eighth (f), half (e) in Form, Flo 229, Trent 89. M. 53, T, rhythm half, quarter, quarter in Verona. M. 55, T, first beat tied eighth (a), eighth (g) in Q 16, Form, Flo 229, G XIII.27, Paris, Trent 89, Trent 91, and Verona. M. 56, C, g', a' in Q 16. M. 59, B, first two beats half-rest in Q 16, Glogauer. Mm. 60–61, C, tie in Q 16, Form, Flo 229, Paris, Verona; B, quarter-note (c) in first beat of m. 61 in G XIII.27, tie and quarter-note (c) in Q 16, Form, Flo 229, Glogauer, Paris, Trent 89, Trent 91, and tie, quarter-note (c), eighth-note (B), eighth-note (A) in first two beats of m. 61 in Seville. Mm. 61–62, T, tie between these measures in Form, Flo 229, G XIII.27, Paris, and Verona. M. 62, C, quarter (g'), eighth (f'), eighth (e'), half (d') in Form, Flo 229, Glogauer, Trent 89; T, first note a in Paris. M. 63, T, quarter (g), eighth (f), eighth (e), half (d) in Form, Flo 229, Glogauer, Trent 89. M. 64, C, last note g' in Q 16. M. 68, B, half-note (d), dotted-half (c), quarter (B) in Form, Flo 229, Trent 89. M. 76, C, quarter (b'), quarter (a'), half (b'), dotted-quarter (a'), eighth (g') in G XIII.27, Paris; T, last note a in Form, Trent 89. Mm. 76–77, C, quarter (b'), quarter (a'), half (b'), dotted-quarter (a'), eighth (g'), barline, dotted-half (g'), quarter (f'), dotted-quarter (f'), eighth (e') in Trent 91. M. 77, C, beats 5–6, quarter (a'), quarter (g') in Q 16 and Seville, dotted-quarter (a'), eighth (g') in Form, Flo 229, G XIII.27, Glogauer, Paris, Trent 89, and Verona. M. 78, C, dotted-half (g'), quarter (f'), quarter (f'), eighth (e'), eighth (f') in Q 16, dotted-half (g'), quarter (e'), half (f') in Glogauer. M. 79, T, half-note, half-rest in Form, Trent 89. M. 80, C, dotted-quarter (d'), eighth (e'), quarter (f'), quarter (e') in Form, Flo 229, G XIII.27, Paris, Seville, Trent 89; B, beat 2 eighth (f), eighth (e) in Glogauer, beat 3 eighth (e) eighth (d) in Paris. Mm. 81-end in three manuscripts, Form, Flo 229, and Trent 89, varies considerably from the other versions. A separate transcription of these measures follows:

Variants to the above example—M. 85, B, whole-note (e-flat) in Trent 89, Form. M. 89, B, beat 1, eighth (f), eighth (e) in Trent 89, Form.

La Martinella (See Nos. 37 and 43.)

23. *La Martinella pittzulo* (à 3)

TRANSCRIPTION—Rome Casanatense 2856, f. 86'–87, "Jo. martini": "la martinellé pittzulo" (i); "La martinella" (i); "La martinellé" (i).

CONCORDANCE—Florence Banco Rari 229, f. 219'–220, Anon.: "(M)artinella" (i); "Martinella" (i); (i).

VARIANTS—M. 10, A, beat 1 half-note (d') in Flo 229. M. 20, A, beat 1 eighth (e'), eighth (d') in Flo 229. M. 25, A, last beat eighth (g'), eighth (f') in Flo 229. M. 44,

T, notated b'-flat in Flo 229. M. 45, B, beats 1 and 2 quarter (d), eighth (c), eighth (B) in Flo 229. M. 46, A, beat 1 eighth (b'), eighth (a') in Flo 229; T, beats 3 and 4 quarter (d"), eighth (c"), eighth (b') in Flo 229. M. 50, B, no notated B-flat in Flo 229.

24. *Le pouverté* (à 3)

TRANSCRIPTION—Rome Casanatense 2856, f. 80'–82, "Jo martini": "Le pouverté" (i); (i); (i).

CONCORDANCE—Verona 757, f. 9'–10, "Jo martini": "La pouverté" (i); (−); (−).

VARIANTS—M. 2, B, beat 2, quarter-note (B) in Verona. M. 3, T, rhythm dotted-half, quarter in Verona. Mm. 5–6, C, dotted-half (g'), quarter (d") tied over barline to quarter (d"), quarter (b'), half (c") in Verona. M. 10, B, notated e-flat in Verona. M. 24, B, notated b-flat in Verona. Mm. 51ff, add to B quarter (G), dotted-quarter (c), eighth (d), quarter (e) tied over barline to eighth (e), eighth (d), half (c), eighth (B), eighth (A), barline, double whole-note (G) in Verona.

Lenchioza mia (See No. 26.)

Les bien amore (See No. 6.)

25. [*Malheur me bat*] (à 3)

TRANSCRIPTION—Florence Banco Rari 229, f. 10'–11, "Janes Mátini": (−); (−); (−).

CONCORDANCES—(a) Bologna Q 16, f. 22'–23 (Arabic foliation), Anon.: "Dieu damors" (i); (i); (i). (b) Bologna Q 18, f. 73'–74, Anon.: "Malur me bat" (i); (i); (i). (c) Egenolff, *Lieder* (RISM c.1535[14]), No. 58, Anon.: "Malheur me bat" (i) (Cantus only). (d) Formschneider, No. 91, Anon.: (−); "Malheur me bat" (i); (−). (e) Petrucci, *Odhecaton A*, f. 68'–69, "Ockenghem": "Malor me bat" (i); (i); (i). (f) Rome Casanatense 2856, f. 57'–59, "Malcort": "Malheur me bat" (i); "Malheur" (i); "Malheur" (i). (g) Rome Giulia XIII.27, f. 72'–73, "Io. Martini": "Malor me bat" (i); (−); (−). (h) St. Gall 461, f. 52–53, "Ockenghem": "Malor me bat" (i); (i); (−).

MODERN EDITIONS—(a) *Ein altes Spielbuch Liber Fridolini Sichery*, ed. Julius Giesbert, p. 60. (b) Josquin de Pres, *Werken*, ed. Albert Smijers, *Missen II*, p. 66. (c) Jacob Obrecht, *Werken*, ed. Johannes Wolf, *Missen I*, pp. 189, 191. (d) Petrucci, *Odhecaton A*, ed. Helen Hewitt, p. 353.

VARIANTS—Mm. 2–3, two whole-notes in Form. M. 3, T, whole-note in Q 18, Form, G XIII.27; CB, whole-note in Q 16, Q 18, Casa, Form, and G XIII.27. Mm. 4–5, C, whole-notes in Form. M. 5, C, whole-note in G XIII.27; T, whole-note in Q 16, Form, G XIII.27; CB, last note c' in Q 16, Q 18, Casa, Form, G XIII.27, Odhecaton A, St. Gall. M. 6, T, beats 1–3 dotted-half in Q 16, Form. M. 7, C, whole-note in Q 16, Form, G XIII.27; T, whole-note in Form, G XIII.27. Mm. 8–12, G XIII.27 reads as follows:

M. 11, CB, half-note (b), quarter-rest, quarter-note (e') in Q 16, Casa, Form, Odhecaton A, St. Gall. M. 13, C, rhythm half, quarter-rest, quarter in Q 16. M. 17, CB, first note erroneously half-note in Flo 229; beats 2 and 3 half-note in Q 16. M. 18, CB, beats 3 and 4 half-note (b) in Q 16. M. 20, C, beat 1, eighth (c"), eighth (b') in Casa, Form, G XIII.27, Odhecaton A, St. Gall; CB, Flo 229 erroneously shows the tied note a' (m. 19, beat 4, and m. 20, beat 1) as only a quarter-note. M. 21, T, beats 1–3 quarter (b) half (e) in Q 18, half (e) quarter (d) in G XIII.27; CB, notated b-flat in Q 18, Casa. M. 22, C, beat 1 quarter (d") in Q 18. M. 23, T, beat 1 quarter (c) in G XIII.27; CB, beat 1 quarter (e) in Q 16, Q 18, Casa, Form, G XIII.27, Odhecaton A, and St. Gall. M. 28, C, rhythm half, half in Odhecaton A, St. Gall; T, beats 1–3 half, quarter in Odhecaton A, St. Gall, dotted-half in Q 16, Casa, Form, G XIII.27; CB, half, half in Odhecaton A, St. Gall. Mm. 28–29, CB, whole tied to whole in Casa. Mm. 28–30, CB, whole tied to whole tied to whole in Q 16, Form. Mm. 29–30, C, rhythm half-rest, half tied over barline to half, half in Q 16, half-rest, half tied over barline to whole in Form. M. 29, CB, whole-note in Odhecaton A, St. Gall. M. 30, C, whole-note in Q 18, G XIII.27. M. 32, C, whole-note in Q 18, Form, G XIII.27; CB, whole-note in Q 16, Q 18, Form. M. 33, C, whole-note in Q 16, Q 18, Form, G XIII.27. Mm. 33–34, T, dotted-quarter (e'), eighth (d'), dotted-quarter (e'), eighth (d'), barline, quarter (b), quarter (c'), eighth (b), eighth (a), eighth (b) in Q 16. M. 35, T, whole-note in Q 16, Casa. Mm. 35–36, T, tie over barline in Q 18. M. 37, CB, dotted-quarter (g), eighth (f), half (d) in Q 18. M. 40, beat 2, quarter (g) in Q 18, Casa, Form, G XIII.27, St. Gall; CB, beat 1, tied eighth (a), eighth (g) in Odhecaton A, St. Gall. M. 42, T, beats 2–3, half-rest in Odhecaton A, St. Gall. M. 43, CB, dotted-half (e), quarter (c) in Q 18. Mm. 44–45, C, tie over barline in Q 18, Form; CB half-rest, half (g) tied over barline to quarter (g), half (a), eighth (g), eighth (f) in Q 16; T, tie over barline in Q 18, Odhecaton A, St. Gall. M. 46, T, beats 1–3 dotted-half in Q 18, Odhecaton A, St. Gall, Form; CB, beats 1 and 2, half (a) in Q 18. M. 47, T, beat 2, eighth (b), eighth (a) in Q 16. M. 49, CB, beats 2 and 3, half-note (a) in Casa. Mm. 50–51, CB, quarter (g), quarter (b), half (a) tied over barline to quarter (a), half (c'), quarter (b) in Casa. M. 51, CB, notated b-flat in Form. M. 55, CB, half-note (a), half-rest in Casa. Mm. 57–58, CB, tied quarter (e'), quarter (d'), quarter (b), quarter (c') tied over barline to quarter (c'), half (b), quarter (a) in Casa. M. 58, C, tied quarter (f'), half (e'), quarter (d') in Casa, tied eighth (f'), eighth (e'), eighth (d'), eighth (c'), half (d') in Q 16; T, beat 2, eighth (f), eighth (e) in Q 16; CB, tied eighth (c'), eighth (b), quarter (a), half (g) in Q 18, Form, tied eighth (c'), eighth (b), eighth (a), eighth (g), half (a) in Q 16, Odhecaton A, St. Gall. Mm. 43–58, G XIII.27 varies greatly. A separate transcription is given below:

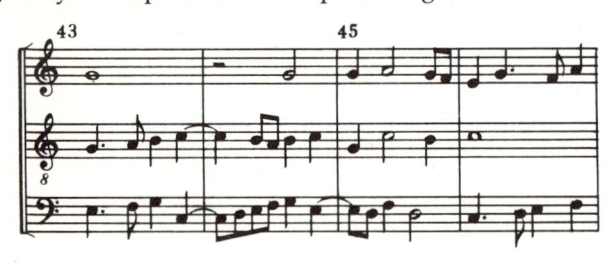

Martinella (See No. 22, "La Martinella," No. 37, "Vive, vive," and No. 43, "Sol fa mi fa sol.")

26. *Nenciozza mia* (à 4)
 TRANSCRIPTION—Petrucci, *Canti C*, f. 101'–102, "Jo. martini": "Nenccioza" (i); (i); (i).
 CONCORDANCE—Seville 5-I-43, f. 130'–131, Anon.: "Lenchioza mia lenchioza balarina" (i); text; "Lenchioza mia lenchioza" (i); "lenchioza mia" (i). The text underlaid in this edition is from the Seville manuscript.
 MODERN EDITION—Martini, *Magnificat e Messe*, ed. Disertori, p. 86.

VARIANTS—Mm. 1–2, C, dotted-half (c''), quarter (b'), barline, quarter (a'), quarter (g'), half (a') in Seville. Mm. 3–4, T, no tie in Seville. M. 11, T, half-note, half-note in Seville. M. 12, CT, Seville erroneously gives d'' as half-note. Mm. 12–13, T, no tie in Seville. M. 16, C, rhythm quarter, quarter, quarter, quarter in Seville. M. 20, B, beat 2 quarter (e) in Seville. M. 24, C, tied eighth (f'), eighth (d'), eighth (d'), eighth (c'), dotted-quarter (b), eighth (a) in Seville. M. 28, T, d'', d'' in Seville. M. 33, T, half (b), half (a), half (a) in Seville. Mm. 34–35, T, no tie in Seville.

27. *Non per la* (à 3)
 TRANSCRIPTION (unicum)—Rome Casanatense 2856, f. 84'–85, "Jo martini": "Non per la" (i); (i); (i).

28. *Non seul uno* (à 4)
 TRANSCRIPTION (unicum)—Rome Casanatense 2856, f. 157'–159, "Jo martini": "Non seul uno" (i); (i); (i); (i).

O di prudenza fonte (See No. 29.)

O intemerata (See No. 5.)

29. *Per faire tousjours* (à 3)
 TRANSCRIPTION—Rome Casanatense 2856, f. 95'–96, "Jo martini": "Per faire tousjours" (i); "Per faire" (i); "Per faire" (i).
 CONCORDANCES—(a) Florence Banco Rari 229, f. 6'–7, "Jañes mátini": "O Diprudéza fóte" (i); (—); (i). (b) Verona 757, f. 27'–28, Anon.: (—); (—); (—).
 VARIANTS—M. 7, B, notated b-flat in Flo 229, Verona. M. 26, C, beats 2 and 3 dotted-quarter (a'), eighth (g') in Flo 229, Verona. M. 31, B, beat 2 eighth (e), eighth (f) in Flo 229, Verona. M. 33, T, beat 2 eighth (e'), eighth (f') in Flo 229, Verona. M. 46, T, beats 1 and 2 quarter (g'), eighth (f'), eighth (e') in Flo 229, Verona.

30. *Que je fasoye* (à 3)
 TRANSCRIPTION (unicum)—Rome Casanatense 2856, f. 133'–134, "Jo Martini": "Que ie fasoye" (i); (i); (i).

31. *Sans siens du mal* (à 3)
 TRANSCRIPTION (unicum)—Rome Casanatense 2856, f. 115'–117, "Jo martini": "Sans siens du mal" (i); (i); (i).

Se la sans plus (See No. 3.)

Se mai il cielo (See No. 19.)

Seruitur (See No. 43.)

32. *Tant que dieu vosdra* (à 3)
 TRANSCRIPTION—Rome Casanatense 2856, f. 98'–100, "Jo martini": "Tant que dieu vosdra" (i); "Tant q̃" (i); "Tant q̃ dieu" (i).

Concordances—(a) Florence Banco Rari 229, f. 2'–3, "Jā̃nes mātini": (–); (–); (–). (b) Verona 757, f. 10'–11, Anon.: (–); (–); (–).

Variants—M. 17, A, rest missing in Verona. M. 29, A, beat 4, quarter-note (g') in Flo 229. M. 31, A, note 2, a' in Flo 229. M. 32, B, rhythm quarter-rest, quarter, quarter, quarter in Flo 229, Verona. M. 41, A, quarter (b), quarter (g), dotted-quarter (c'), eighth (b) in Casa. M. 43, T, d as half-note in error in Verona.

33. *Tousjours bien* (à 3)

Transcription (unicum)—Rome Casanatense 2856, f. 108'–109, "Jo martini": "Tousjours bien" (i); (i); (i).

Modern edition—Oscar Chilescott, "'Tousjours bien' di Jo. Martini," in *Revista musicale italiana* XXIII (1916), pp. 66.

34. *Tousjours me souviendra* (à 3)

Transcription (unicum)—Rome Casanatense 2856, f. 131'–132, "Jo Martini": "Tous iours me souviendra" (i); "Tousjours" (i); "Tousjours" (i).

35. *Tout joyeulx* (à 3)

Transcription (unicum)—Rome Casanatense 2856, f. 117'–118, "Jo. martini": "Tout joyeulz" (i); (i); "Tót joyeulx" (i).

Variant—M. 9, B, last note B (error?) in Casa.

36. *Tres doulx regart* (à 4)

Transcription—Petrucci, *Canti C*, f. 114'–115, Anon.: "Tres doulx regart" (i); "Tres doulx" (i); "Tres doulx" (i), "Tres doulx" (i).

Concordance—Found in Florence Banco Rari 229, f. iv–v, in three parts only, no title, but attributed to "Jannes Martini." See and compare No. 38, "do si la sol la."

37. *Vive, vive* (à 3)

Transcription—Rome Casanatense 2856, f. 28'–29, "Jo martini": "vive vive" (i); (i); (i).

Concordances—(a) Florence Banco Rari 229, f. 44'–45, Anon.: "Martinella" (i); (i); (i). (b) Seville 5-I-43, f. 28'–29, Anon.: "(G)arde(s) vous donc" (i); (i); (i).

Variants—M. 3, B, no notated e-flat in Seville. M. 4, T, beat 1 eighth (a), eighth (g) in Flo 229, Seville. M. 7, T, notated e'-flat in Flo 229, Seville. M. 8, A, beat 1 eighth (a'), eighth (g') in Flo 229, Seville. Mm. 12–14, T and B, read as follows in Flo 229, Seville:

M. 16, T, c' whole-note (error), other values remain constant, in Seville. M. 18, B, beats 3–4, dotted-quarter (g), eighth (a) in Flo 229 and Seville. M. 19, B, beats 1 and 2, quarter (b), quarter (c') in Flo 229, Seville. Mm. 21–24, A, reads as follows in Flo 229, Seville:

M. 22, B, beats 1–2, eighth (e), eighth (d), eighth (c), eighth (B) in Flo 229, Seville. M. 23, A, quarter (g), dotted-quarter (b), eighth (a), quarter (d') with tie in Seville for excerpt quoted above. M. 30, B, tied eighth (f), eighth (e), quarter (d), half (g) in Flo 229, Seville. Mm. 31–32, B, quarter-rest, quarter (g), quarter (e), quarter (a) tied over barline to eighth (a), eighth (g), half (g), quarter (f) in Flo 229, Seville. M. 34, A, beats 3–4, dotted-quarter (e'), eighth (f') in Flo 229, Seville. M. 45, B, no notated e-flat in Seville. Mm. 46–47, B, no tie over barline, quarter-note (g) on beat 1 of m. 47 in Flo 229, Seville. M. 47, A, beat 1 eighth (a'), eighth (g') in Seville.

38. *Do si la sol la* (à 3)

Transcription—Florence Banco Rari 229, f. iv–v, "Jannes Martini": (–); (–); (–).

Concordance—See and compare No. 36, "Tres doulx regart" (à 4).

39. *Re mi fa sol la* (à 3)

Transcription (unicum)—Florence Banco Rari 229, f. 216'–217, "Jannes Martini": (–); (–); (–).

40. *Re fa sol la la* (à 4)

Transcription (unicum)—Florence Banco Rari 229, f. 173'–174, "Jannes Martini": (–); (–); (–); (–).

41. *Fa mi re do re* (à 3)

Transcription—Florence Banco Rari 229, f. 8'–9, "Jā̃nes mātini": (–); (–); (–).

42. *Sol mi fa sol sol* (à 3)

Transcription (unicum)—Florence Banco Rari 229, f. 235'–236, "Jannes Martini": (–); (–); (–).

43. *Sol fa mi fa sol* (à 3) (Martinella)

Transcription—Rome Casanatense 2856, f. 138'–140, Anon.: "Martinella" (i); (i); (i).

Concordances—(a) Paris Vm^{7}676, f. 36'–37, Anon.: "Seruitur" (i); (i); (i). (b) Rome Cappella Giulia XIII.27, f. 68'–69, Anon.: "La martinella" (i); (i); (i). (c) Formschneider (1538[9]), No. 35, Anon.: (–); (–); (–). (d) Florence Banco Rari 229, f. 141'–142, Anon.: "Martinella" (i); (i); (i).

Variants—M. 1, B, color in Flo 229. M. 3, T, color in Flo 229. M. 5, B, beat 3, e in G XIII.27, Paris 676, Flo

229; f in Form. Mm. 6–7, T, half (a), half (g), tied over barline to quarter (g), half (b), quarter (e) in Paris 676. M. 8, B, note 3, no flat in Flo 229. M. 10, B, note 1, notated b-flat in G XIII.27, Form. M. 10, beat 4, and m. 11, beat 1, T, no color in G XIII.27, Form. M. 12, T, tie in G XIII.27, Flo 229, Form; B, whole-note in G XIII.27. M. 13, B, beats 1–2, half-rest in G XIII.27. M. 16, B, notes 2–3, rhythm dotted-quarter, eighth in Flo 229. M. 19, T, notes 1–2, quarter (b), eighth (a), eighth (g) in G XIII.27, Paris 676, Form, Flo 229. M. 20, C, note 1, b erroneously written as half-note in Flo 229. M. 23, T, notes 1–2, minor color in G XIII.27, Flo 229. M. 24, T, beat 1, tied eighth (c), eighth (b) in G XIII.27, Paris 676, Form. M. 30, C, beats 2–3, minor color in Flo 229. M. 31, B, beat 4 to m. 32, beat 1, no color in Form, Flo 229. M. 32, B, beats 3–4, minor color in G XIII.27, Flo 229. M. 33, T, beats 1–2, minor color in Flo 229. M. 34, T, quarter (e), half (d), eighth (c), eighth (b) in Flo 229; B, note l is d in G XIII.27; B, note 1 erroneously half-note in Flo 229; C, notes 2–3, minor color in Flo 229. M. 35, T, beats 3–4, minor color in G XIII.27. M. 36, T, beat 4, notated e-flat in Form. M. 38, C, T, B, no corona in G XIII.27. M. 45, T, beat 4 to m. 46, beat 1, T, color in G XIII.27. M. 53, C, beat 4, to m. 55, beat 1, no color in Form. M. 56, B, dotted-quarter (f), sixteenth (e), sixteenth (d), half (c) in Form. M. 57, B, no flat before e in G XIII.27, Paris 676. M. 59, B, beat 3, notated e-flat in Form. M. 60, B, beats 3–4, dotted-quarter, eighth in G XIII.27. M. 61, S, beats 3–4, minor color in G XIII.27. M. 63, C, time signature 3 in Flo 229; half (f'), quarter (g'), quarter (a') in Form; note 2, punctus divisionis in Paris 676. M. 64, C, beats 1–2, triplet consisting of dotted-quarter (b'), eighth (a'), quarter (g') in Form. M. 65, C, beats 3–4, triplet consisting of half (f') tied to eighth (f'), sixteenth (e') in Paris 676, triplet consisting of dotted-quarter (f'), eighth (e'), quarter (f') in Form, Flo 229.

44. *Sol la si do si* (à 3)

TRANSCRIPTION—Florence Banco Rari 229, f. 143'–144, "Jannes Martini": (–); (–); (–).

CONCORDANCE—Verona 757, f. 25'–26, Anon.: (–); (–); (–).

VARIANTS—Verona scribe omitted the passage from the first beat of measure 35 through measure 41 in the Cantus part. The error occurs at the end of one staff line (m. 35), the beginning of the next staff being measure 42. M. 15, B, note 2, eighth (a) in Verona. M. 21, B, dotted-quarter (c), eighth (d), dotted quarter (e), eighth (c) in Verona. M. 22, B, dotted-quarter (f), eighth (g), half (d) in Verona. M. 32, B, beats 1–2, quarter-note, quarter-rest in Verona. M. 46, C, whole-note, (b') in Verona; T, whole-note (d') in Verona; B, whole-note (g) in Verona.

Acknowledgments

Many persons have generously provided assistance, and I express my deepest gratitude for their various kinds of help. Dr. Klaus Speer and Dr. Ruth Watanabe of the Eastman School of Music made available the resources of Sibley Music Library. I especially thank my former secretary, Nancy Wilson, and present secretary, Carol Montgomery, who have typed the manuscript, and those graduate students who checked information and transcriptions.

I am also indebted to Renaissance scholars, among whom I would name Thomas Noblitt, Howard Mayer Brown, Ludwig Finscher, Arthur Wolff, John Brawley, Lewis Lockwood, and Theodore Karp.

For providing information, making microfilms available, and permitting direct access to sources, the following libraries, through appropriate administrative officers, offered valuable, much needed services: Basel, Universitätsbibliothek; Bologna, Civico Museo Bibliografico Musicale; Florence, Biblioteca Nazionale Centrale; Paris, Bibliothèque Nationale; Perugia, Biblioteca Comunale; Rome, Biblioteca Casanatense; St. Gall, Stiftsbibliothek; Seville, Biblioteca Columbina; Vatican, Biblioteca Apostolica Vaticana; Verona, Biblioteca Capitolare.

Edward G. Evans, Jr.
University of Connecticut
Storrs, Connecticut

August, 1975

Notes

[1] Antonio Cappelli, "Notizie di Ugo Caleffini con la sua cronaca in rima di Casa d'Este," *Atti e memorie della RR. Deputazioni de Storia Patria per la Provincie Modenesi e Parmensi* (Modena, 1867), Series I, Vol. 2, p. 286.

[2] Adriano Cappelli, "La Biblioteca Estense nella prima meta del secolo XV," *Giornale Storico della Letternatura Italiano* (Modena, 1867), Series I, Vol. 2, pp. 12–30.

[3] Angelo Camillo Decembrio, *Politiae Litterariae Angeli Decembrii Mediolanensis, oratoris clarissimi, ad summum Pontificem Pium II, libri septem* (Augsburg, 1540), I, p. 6 et passim.

[4] Gustave Gruyer, *L'art ferrarais à l'époque des princes d'Este* (Paris, 1897), I, pp. 23–35.

[5] Johannes Ferrariensis, "Excerpta ex Annalium Libris illustris Familiae Marchioun Estensium, 1409–1454," *Rerum Italicarum Scriptores*, edited by Locovico Antonio Muratori (Bologna, reprinted 1925), Vol. XX, col. 456.

[6] Johannes Ferrariensis, *op. cit.*, cols. 466–472.

[7] Antonio Cornazano, *Il Libro dell'arte del danzare di Antonio Cornazano*, reprinted in Florence, 1915, also edited by C. Mazzi, in *La Bibliofilia*, XVII (1916), p. 10.

Chi uole passare da un mundo a l'altro,
Odi sonare pierobono.
Chi uole trouare el cielo aperto,
Proui la liberalità del Ducha Borso.
Chi uole uedere el paradiso in terra,
Ueggi Madonna Beatrice in una festa.

Pietro Bono, celebrated lutenist, lived at the Neapolitan court of Ferrante, was later associated with Borso and Ercole I at Ferrara (until 1488), briefly served Beatrice, daughter of Ferrante and wife of Matthias Corvinus, King of Hungary, but finally returned to live in Ferrara until his death. The Beatrice of this poem is most likely Ferrante's daughter. Both she and her sister, Leonora, who married Ercole I, had been taught music by Tinctoris and were skilled players on several instruments, among them the lute.

[8] Giulio Bertoni, *La Biblioteca Estense e la coltura Ferrarese ai tempi del Duca Ercole I (1471–1505)* (Torino, 1903), pp. 235–252.

[9] Thomas Noblitt, Ludwig Finscher, Theodore Karp, Howard Brown, John Brawley, and Arthur Wolff have kindly given much assistance over a period of years. More recently, Lewis Lockwood has graciously shared his findings, among which was information on Martini's last years and death, information which had hitherto eluded the efforts of all other scholars. The following entries are obviously highly selective:

Barblan, Guglielmo, "Vita musicale alla corte Sforzesca," in *Storia di Milano* (Fondazione Treccani degli Alfieri, Milan, 1961), Vol. IX.

Bertolotti, Antonio, *Musici alla corte dei Gonzaga in Mantova del secolo XV al XVIII, notizie e documenti raccolti negli Archivi Mantovani* (Milano, 1890).

Bertoni, Giulio, see fn. 8.

Brawley, John, "The Magnificats, Hymns, Motets, and Secular Compositions of Johannes Martini," (Ph.D. dissertation, Yale University, 1968). University Microfilms, No. 69–8321.

Davari, Stefano, "La musica a Mantova: notizie biografiche di maestri di musica, cantori e suonatori presso la Corte di Mantova," *Rivista storica mantovana* (1885), Vol I.

Disertori, Benvenuto, *Johannes Martini, Magnificat e Messe*, Archivium Musices Metropolitanum Mediolanese (Veneranda Fabbrica del Duomo di Milano, Milan, n.d.).

Finscher, Ludwig, "Martini, Johannes," *MGG*, Vol. 8, cols. 1723–1726.

Karp, Theodore, "The Secular Works of Johannes Martini," *Aspects of Medieval and Renaissance Music: A Birthday Offering to Gustave Reese* (New York, 1966), pp. 455–473.

Lockwood, Lewis, article on Martini to be published in the forthcoming edition of *Grove's Dictionary of Music and Musicians*.

Lockwood, Lewis, "Music at Ferrara in the Period of Ercole I d'Este," *Studi Musicali* (Florence, 1972), Vol. I, No. 1, pp. 101–131.

Morselli, Antonia, "Ippolito I d'Este e il suo primo viaggio in Ungheria (1487)," *Atti e Memorie dell'Accademia di Scienza, Lettere ed Arti di Modena* (1957), Ser. V, Vol. XV, pp. 196, 251.

Motta, Emilio, "Musici alla carte degli Sforza," *Archivio storico lombardo* (Milano, 1887), serie seconda, Vol. IV, Anno XIV, pp. 514–561.

Noblitt, Thomas, "The Magnificats of Johannes Martini," in *Paul A. Pisk, Essays in His Honor* (Austin, 1966), pp. 10–24.

Reese, Gustave, *Music in the Renaissance* (New York, 1954), pp. 220–223.

Valdrighi, Luigi, "Cappelle, concerti e musiche di casa d'Este (dal sec. XV al XVIII)," *Atti e memorie delle regie deputazioni ai storia patria per le provincie modenesi e parmense*. Ser. III, Vol. II (1883), pp. 415–495.

Wolff, Arthur S., "The Chansonnier Biblioteca Casanatense 2856, Its History, Purpose, and Music," (Ph.D. dissertation, North Texas State University, 1970). University Microfilms, No. 71–8696.

[10] Finscher, *op. cit.*, col. 1725; Reese, *op. cit.*, p. 221 (Chapter heading, "Josquin des Pres and His Contemporaries"); Karp, *op. cit.*, pp. 459–460.

[11] Jacques de Meyere, *Rerum Flandricarum, Tomi X* (Antwerp, 1531), in *Recueil de chroniques, chartes et autres documents concernant l'histoire et les antiquités de la Flandre* (Bruges, 1843), Ser. II, p. 83.

Testes sunt... Thomas Martinus cum fratribus Petro ac Joanne, patria Armenterius....

[12] Luigi F. Valdrighi, *op. cit.*, p. 443.

Ad. D. hermanum Episcopum Constantienum. Reverendus in Christo pater et domine pater noster dilectissime. Inter ceteras provisiones quas facere cepimus in principio nostre assumptionis ad hunc nostrum ducatum, statuimus pro nostra Spirituali recreatione, Instituere Capellam celeberrimam, in qua ad divinum cultum et officia celebranda habeamus Cantores Musicos prestantissimos, quos undique perquirimus. Qua de re cum ad noticiam nostram pervenerit de sufficentia, integritate, ac vita honestate ven. lis domini Martini de Alemania, Sacerdotis in ecclesia cathedrali V.D. et habita per nos informatione quod in arte Musica plurimum valet, ipsum in cantorem capelle nostre predicte delegimus atque conduximus. Quapropter vestram R.P. ex corde regamus ut eadem velit intuitu et amore nostro acquiescere et contentarj ut ipse D. Martinus Loco suj ponere et subrogare possit alium idoneum qui curam habeat celebrandi et Gubernandi beneficium suum quod habet in ecclesia maiorj Constan: nec non velit ipsa D. Vestra se interponere cum Capitulo et venerabilibus illis Canonicis ecclesie predicte, ut et ipsi huic voto nostro libenter annuantur Quum id a vestra Rev. P. et a suis Reverent... Item predicto D. Martino facte fuerunt littere passum prose et uno sotio vel famulo et cum duobus equis, pro eundo constantiam et redeundo.

[13] Lockwood, "Music at Ferrara," p. 117, fn. 45.

[14] Archivio di Stato, *Potenze Sovrane*, p. 154. See Guglielmo Barblan, "Vita musicale alla corte Sforzesca," *Storia di Milano* (Milano, 1961), Vol. IX, pp. 813–814.

...Gratam habentes collationem quam fecistis presbitero Iohanni de Alamania, organiste in ecclesia vestra, de capellis nuncupatis altera scilicet illorum de Bastardis, et altera illorum de Tonsis.

[15]Lockwood, "Music at Ferrara," p. 117, fn. 45.
[16]Passport reproduced in Barblan, *op. cit.* p. 825.
[17]Motta, *op. cit.*, p. 323.

Cantori de cappella.

d. Abbate	ducati	xiiij	Jacheto de Rohano	ducati	viij
d. Bovis	"	xij	d. lo Preosto	"	viij
d. Andrea	"	xij	d. Ghineto	"	vij
d. Zoanne da Vignon	"	xij	Michele da Torsi	"	v
Raynaldino	"	xij	Aluyseto	"	v
Car.le	"	x	Zohanne Martino	"	v
Cornelio	"	x	Juschino	"	v
Michele de Feys	"	x	el fratello del Abbà	"	v
c. Zohanne Cornuel	"	x	d. Raynero	"	iiij
Perotino	"	x	Antonio Ponso	"	x
Thebaldo	"	x	Alexandro	"	x

[18]Lockwood, "Music at Ferrara," p. 118, fn. 48.
[19]*El Escorial* MS C.iii.23, 6f.

Esta es sciencia asi en el modo del componer commo del cantar y tañer que dudo si los advenideros podran pasar mas adelante quanto toca estas tres cosas que son: componer, cantar y tanner en todos los instrumentos del mundo. Non dudo, que non aya algunas cosas nuevas en las invenciones, della mas no que mas sotilmente puedan hordenar nin discantar el contrapunto conpuesto por mui doctas y singulares personas, donde fueron: dustable, dufay, ihohannes okeghem, maestro de capilla del rey de francia, binchois, constas, busnois, vuillelmus faugueus, enricus thil'r, pulois, johannes utrreode, johannes martini.

[20]Consult Lockwood article for *Grove's*; Brawley, *op. cit.*, pp. 15, 16; Disertori, *op. cit.*, i–iii, ix.
[21]Valdrighi, *op. cit.*; Brawley, *op. cit.*, pp.151–156; Ludwig Fökövi, "Musik und musikalische Verhältnisse in Ungarn am Hofe von Mattias Corvinus," *Kirchenmusikalisches Jahrbuch* (1900), Vol. XV, pp. 15–16.
[22]Fökövi, *op. cit.*, p. 15.

Illustrissime ac Excellentissime Princeps et Domine Domine Singularissime, perche quello organista de questa Serenissima Regina chiamato Danielle, il quale a li di passati fu a Vostra Excellentia e novamente morto. La Maesta Sua mi have comisso, che per parte de quella pregi Vostra Excellentia volgi mandare Zohane Martino musico suo ne la magna a ritrovare uno mastro Paulo organista il quale serve il Duca Sigismondo, che se nomina de austria, et cometerli, che parendoli, che il non silgij, inferiore al prefato Daniele morto in quella arte, vedi per ogni modo menargelo li a Ferrara, et havendolo Vostra Excellentia et trovandolo disposto al servire Sua Maesta, ge ne dagi subito adviso, on accadendoli comoditate de avarigello, ge lo avij.

Budc 26 septembris 1489

[23]*Archivio Gonzaga*, Mantova.

Illustrissime et potens donna. Lo illustrissimo signor duca nostro me ha decto et comesso che io debia venire a vostra signoria per alcuni giorni per insignare a vostra signoria cantare et Io lo voglio fare molto volentiera et de bon core. Ma perche el tempo me strenge parte a provedere ali bisogni de la casa et parte per altre occurente neccessita, priego et supplico a vostra signoria quella sia contenta aspectare per di quindexe acio che io posse provedere ali mei bisogni, et dapoi subito veniro a vostra signoria et aquella satisfaro quanto a mi sia possibile, et piu che volentieri aspecto la risposta de vostra signoria et aquella mi ricomando per mille fiate. Vale etc. etc. 2° septembre 1490.

Servitor Joanes Martinus
Cantor illustrissimi domini ducis etc.

[24]*Archivio Gonzaga*, Mantova.

Illustrissime et excellentissime domine domine marchionisse etc.

Io mande uno cantzon a la vostre signoria per darne qualque recreation et se recorde ala signoria vostra che cantadi spesse per pilere bene le pratica. Semper me recomande a la signoria vostra. Data a Ferrare a 18 dii avril 1491.

Don J. Martin
Cantor semper servitor.

[25]Lockwood, "Music at Ferrara," p. 119, fn. 50, states that Anna Maria Sforza wrote to Cardinal Ippolito (Este) asking for a benefice for a favorite of hers which is held by "Zoanne Martino Cantore quando il caso de la morte sua accadesse...." On December 29, 1497, Ercole writes of benefices which had already been vacated by Martini's death, thus: "Inanti che vacassano li benefitij de Zoanne martino nostro cantore per la morte sua..." (*Archivio di Stato*, Modena, Carteggio tra Principi Estensi, B. 140 and B. 69/9). Lockwood's discovery represents the first certain evidence of Martini's approximate death date. Writers prior to Lockwood could only hazard a date "after 1492."
[26]Found in Florence Banco Rari 229, f. 143'–144, and Segovia, f. 197'–198.
[27]Karp, *op. cit.*, pp. 463–464, briefly compares Mass sections with their counterparts in the chanson. Out of seventeen sections, all but four contain borrowings from the secular piece.
[28]Wolff, *op. cit.* This study is by far the most important and most extensive on the Casanatense manuscript. After thoroughly describing the physical features of the manuscript, Wolff systematically establishes a plausible explanation of its origin (*ca.* 1485) and later history. His arguments which relate Casanatense 2856 to the joining of the Este and Gonzaga families are convincing.
[29]According to Edward Lowinsky, Howard M. Brown's study will eventually be published as Volumes 7 and 8 of *Monuments of Renaissance Music*.
[30]Wolff, *op. cit.*, p. 25.
[31]Jose M.ª Llorens, "El Codice Casanatense 2.856 identificado como el Cancionero de Isabella d'Este (Ferrara), espose de Francesco Gonzaga (mantua)," *Anuario musical*, XX (1965), p. 169.
[32]Anne Bragard, "Un manuscrit Florentin du quattrocento: Le Magl. XIX. 59 (B.R. 220)," *Revue de Musicologie*, LII (1966), p. 59.
[33]Lockwood, article for *Grove's*; Brown, *Monuments* (see fn. 29 above).
[34]Gustave Reese, *Music in the Renaissance* (New York: W. W. Norton and Company, Inc., 1954), Plate III.
[35]Formschneider, *Trium vocum carmina* (RISM 1538[9]), No. 36.
[36]The piece is notated in tablature with the words "Isacio compositori." A transcription can be found in Brawley, pp. 197–199.
[37]The textless pieces are Nos. 38–42 and 44 of this edition.
[38]Brawley, *op. cit.*, pp. 77–83.
[39]Bertoni, *op. cit.*, p. 260.

Un libro da canto, figurat che scripse e notò Don Alessandro Signorello a la pifaresca, con un principio miniato all'antica, con l'arma Ducale e con lettere d'oro a l'antica.

[40]See fn. 17; also Reese, *op. cit.*, p. 220.
[41]Ludwig Finscher, *Loyset Compère: Life and Works* (American Institute of Musicology, 1964).
[42]Brawley, *op. cit.*, p. 64.
[43]Bianca Becherini, *Catalogo dei manoscritti musicali della Biblioteca Nazionale di Firenze* (Kassel: Bärenreiter, 1959), p. 76.
[44]Oliver Strunk, *Source Readings in Music History* (New York: W. W. Norton and Company, Inc., 1950), p. 214, fn. m and p. 206, fn. 1.
[45]Wolff, *op. cit.*, p. 43, fn. 9.
[46]Brawley, *op. cit.*, pp. 73–75.
[47]Wolff, *op. cit.*, p. 49.
[48]Charlotte Greenspan, "The chansons of Johannes Martini" (Master's thesis, University of Illinois, 1964).
[49]Brawley, *op cit.*, Chapters V and VI.
[50]Karp, *op. cit.*, pp. 461–472.

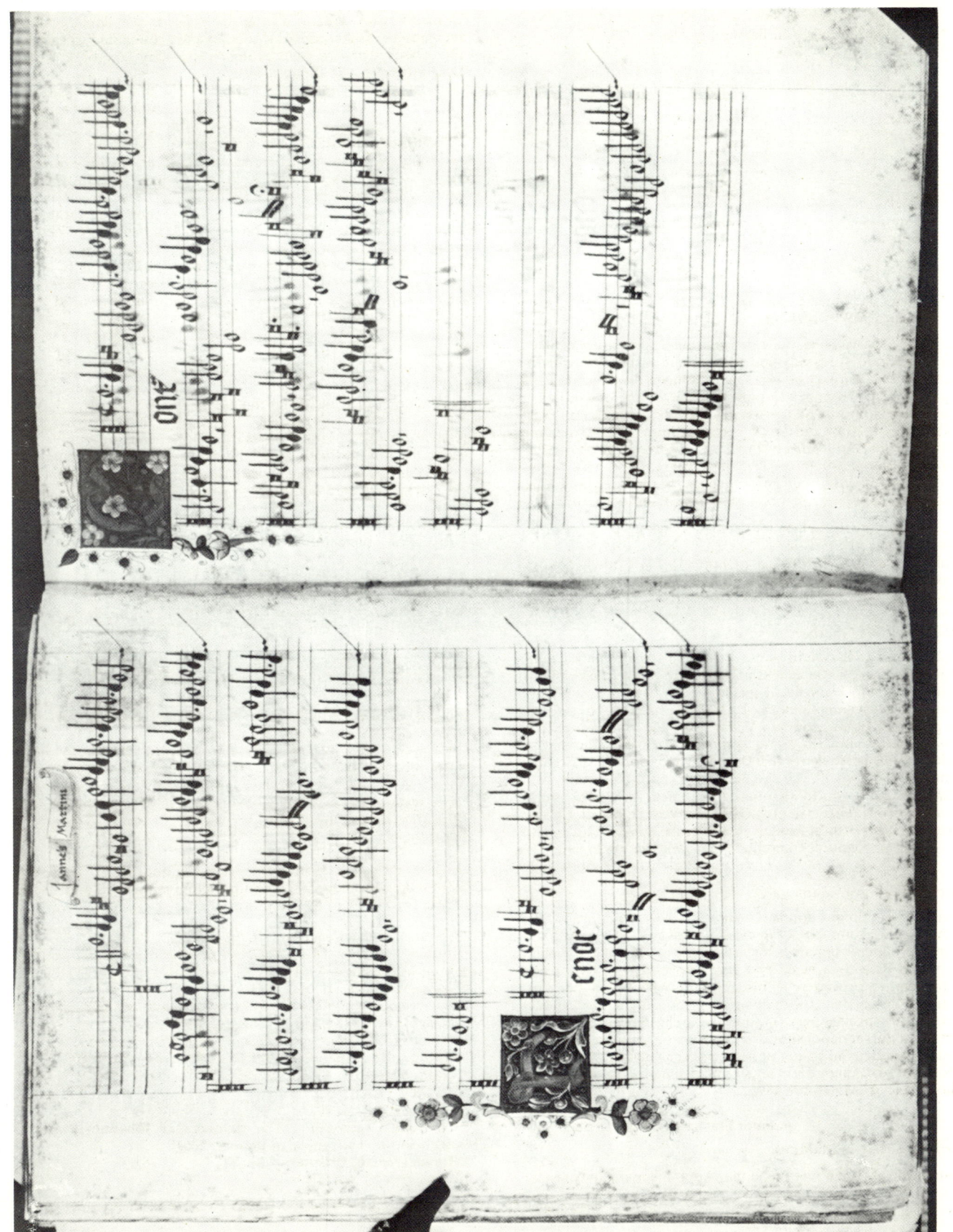

Plate I. ["Il est tousjours"], Florence Banco Rari 229, f.16ʳ–17.

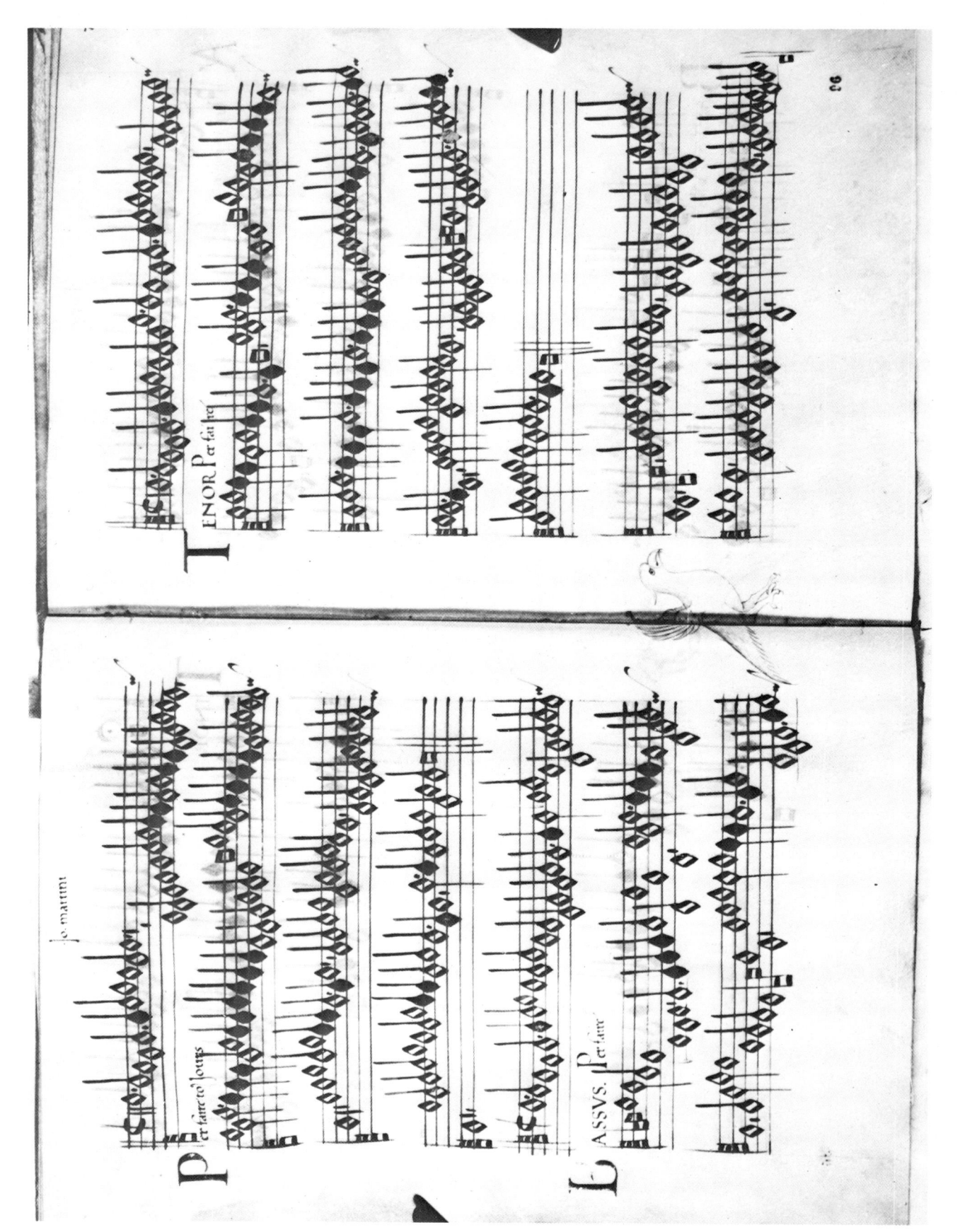

Plate II. "Per faire tousjours," Rome Casanatense 2856, f. 95'–96.

SECULAR PIECES

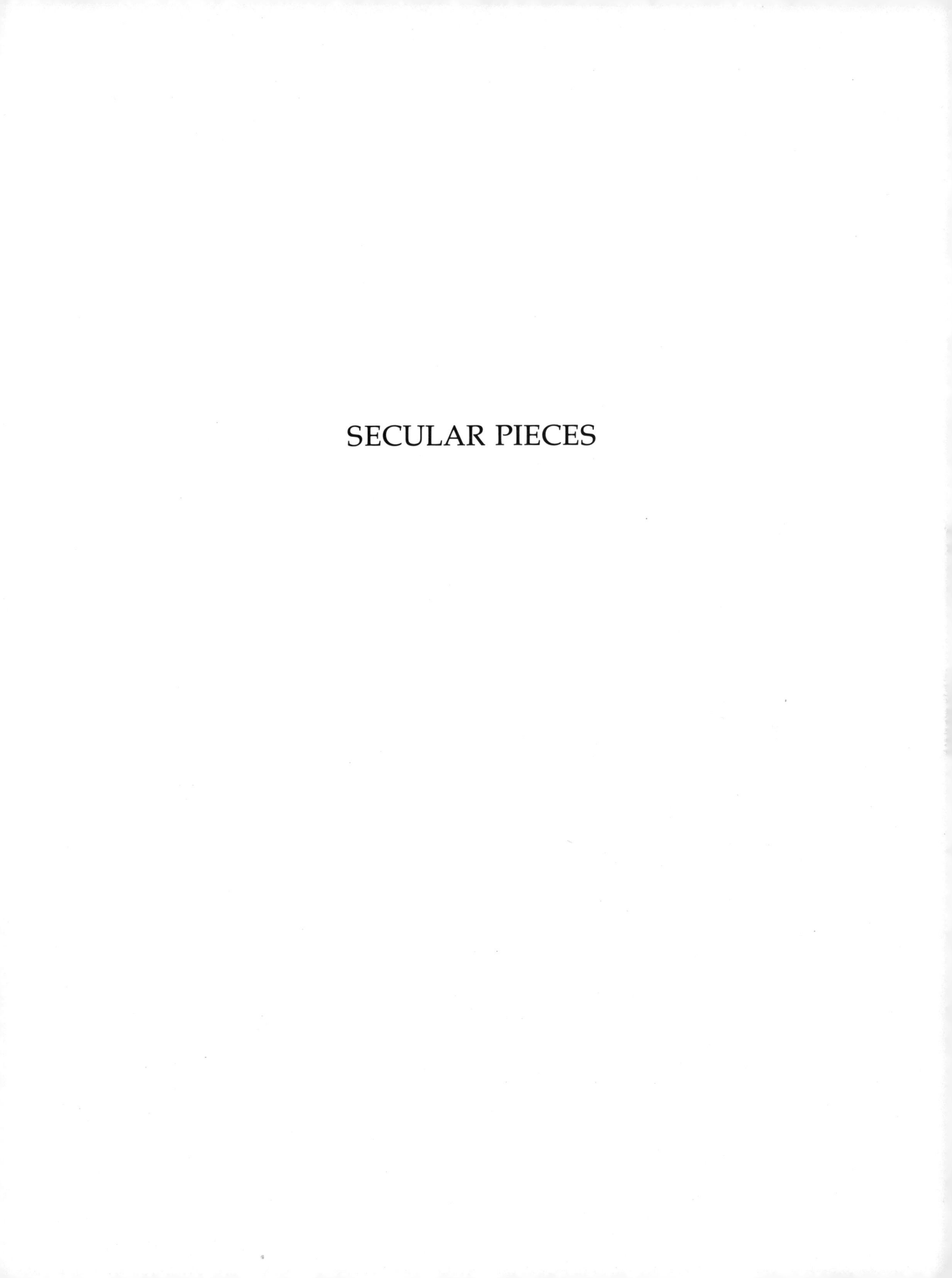

Biaulx parle tousjours

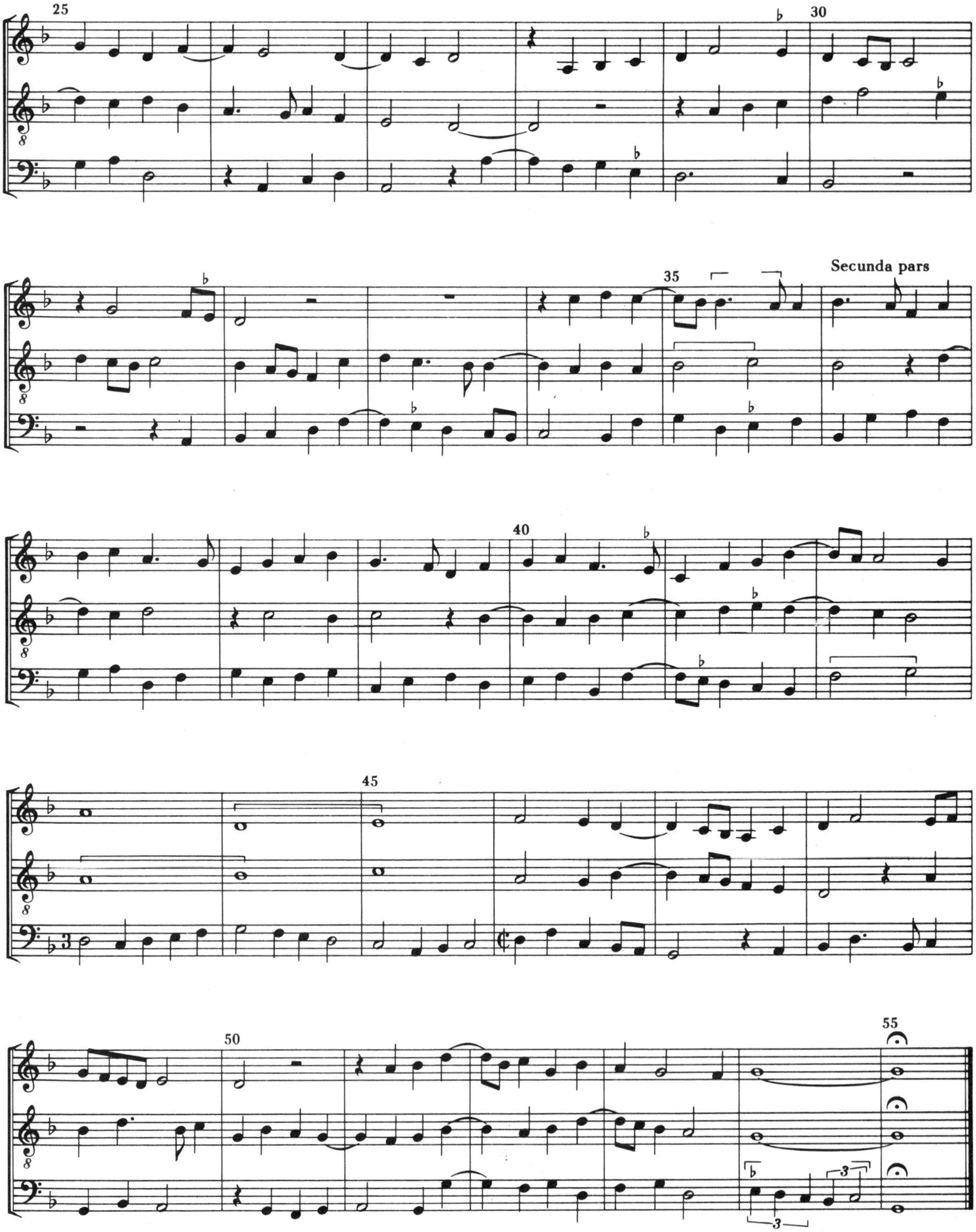
25
30
35
Secunda pars
40
45
50
55

Cayphas

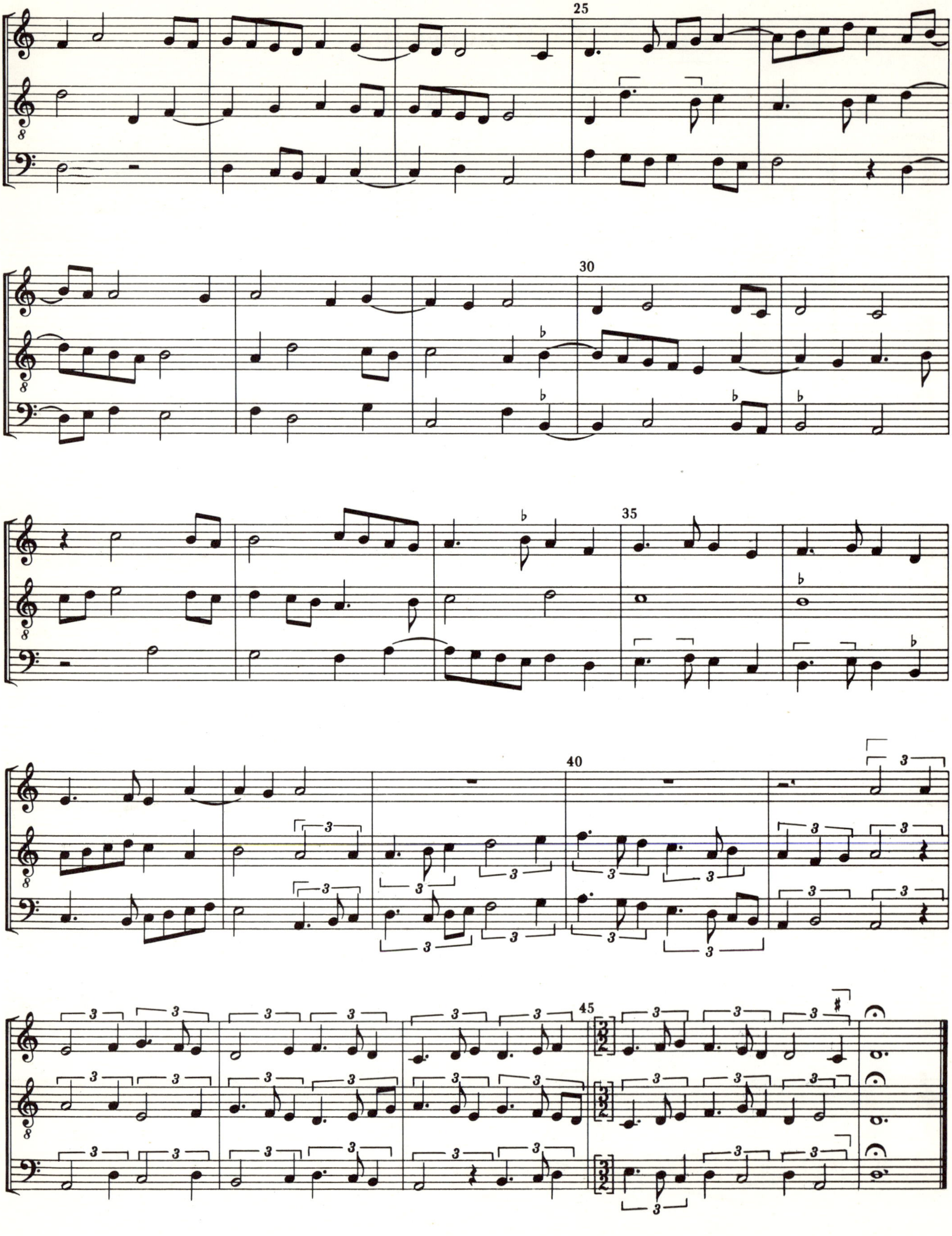
25
30
35
40
45

Cela sans plus

20
-ra bel- la de bon re- bom, Je-
bre- - gie- ra bel- la de bon re- bom,
25
30
-tes mon cor hors de vous pri- son, vous
Je-
35
pri- son,
-tes mon cor hors de vous pri-

De la bonne chiere

8

[Der newe pawir schwantcz]

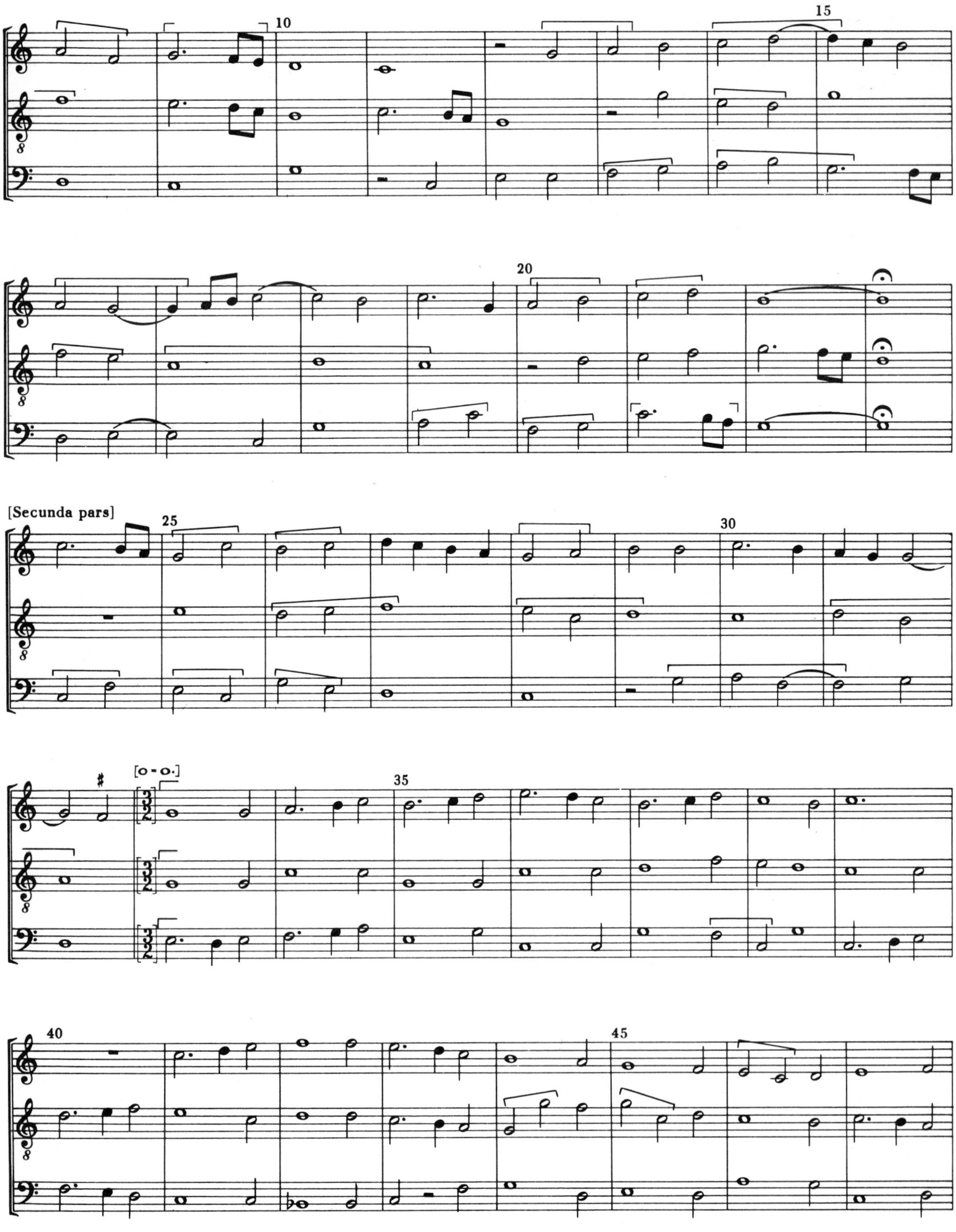
10
15
20
[Secunda pars]
25
30
[o = o.]
35
40
45

Des biens d'amours
Version A

[Secunda pars]

Des biens d'amours
Version B

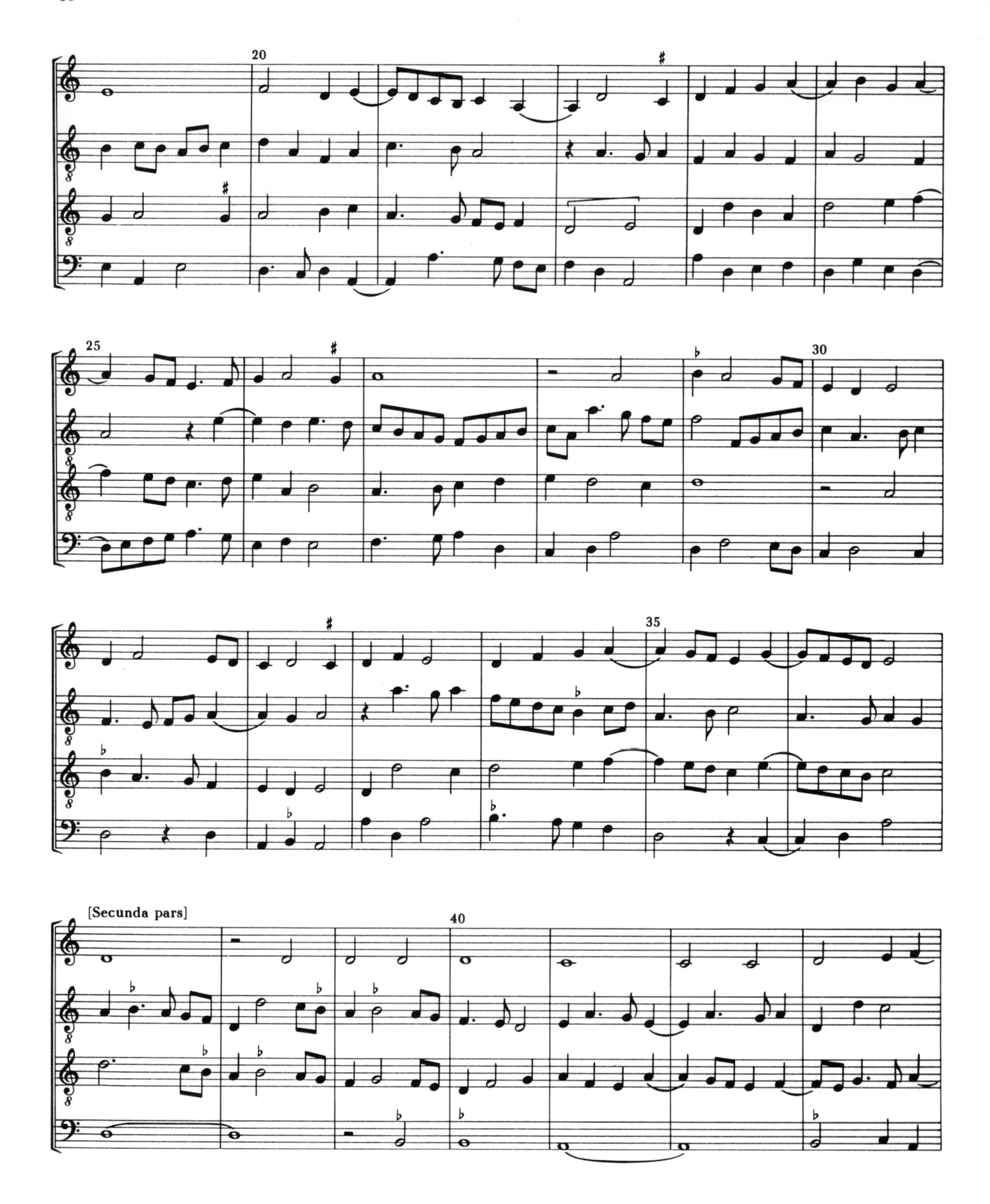
20
25
30
35
[Secunda pars]
40

Fault il que heur soye

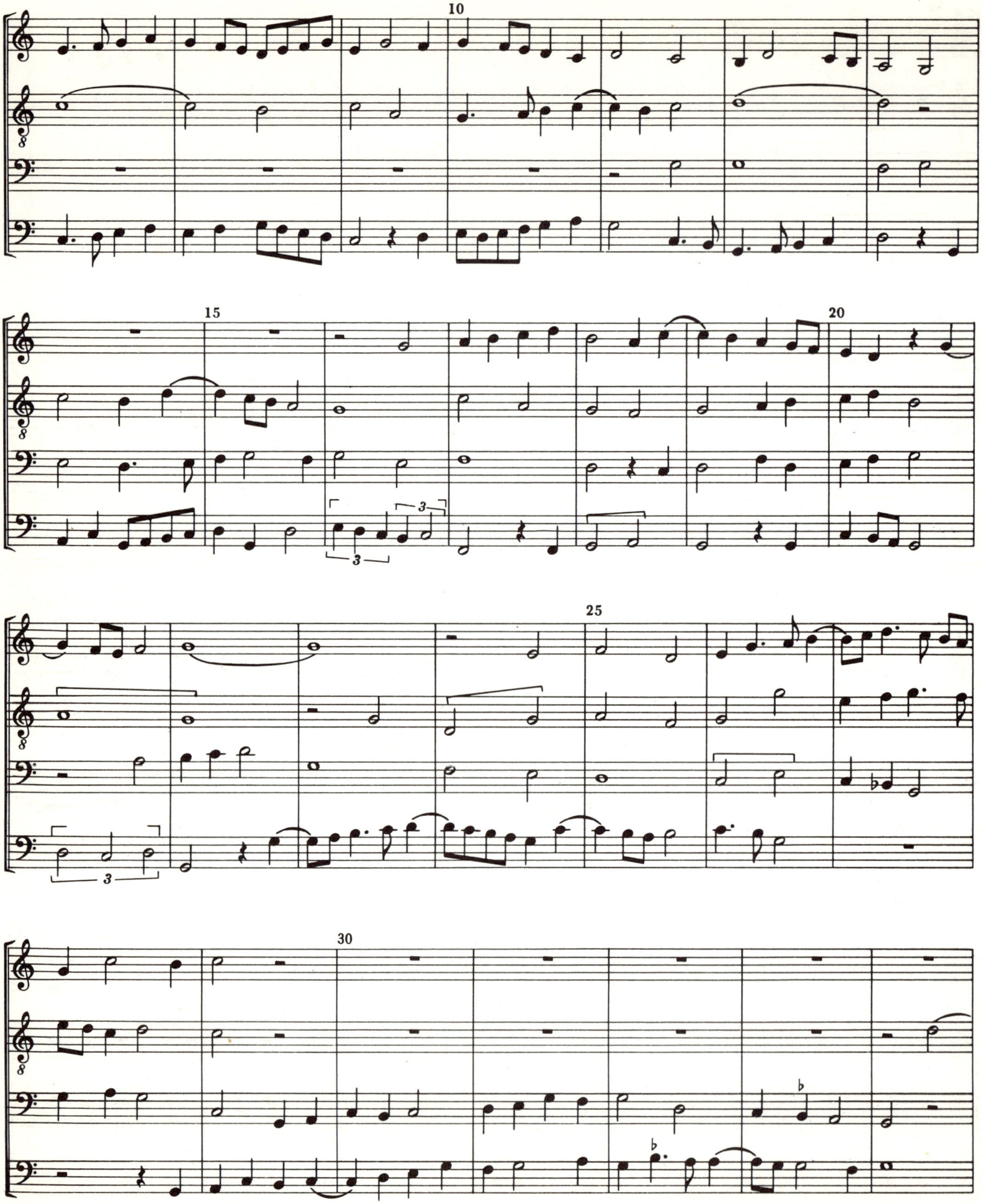
10
15
20
25
30

17

18

Fortuna desperata

25
e ma- le- de- ta che- - - de
30
Secunda pars
35
tal do- na e- - le- - -
40
-ta la fa- ma ay de-
45
-ne ga- - - - - -

Fortuna d'un gran tempo

15
20
leg - gi - a - - dra Gra - ti - o - sa e
Tan - to leg - gia - dra Gra -ti - o - sae bel - la,
25
bel - - - - la,
So - lo un - a gra - ti -
30
So - lo un - a gra - ti - a tag - gi - o
-a tag - gio a di - man-da - ta,
Ed a - quel -

a di - man - da - ta, Ed a - quel - la mi - se sta -
-la mi - se sta - ta ri - bel - la.
-ta ri - bel - - la. E chi lo vuol sa - pe -
E chi lo vuol sa - pe - re si lo
-re si lo sap - - pi - a, In que - sta ter -
sap - pi - a, In que - sta ter - ra vog - lio be ne

60
-ra vog-lio be ne a - du - na, Un-
a - du - na,
65
-de gli fu- a a man- ti- mi- mi- nac- ci - a, Cre - den -
Un - de gli fu- a a - man - ti mi mi- nac-ci- a,
70
- do chi - o la la - sei per pav - ra.
75
Cre-den-do chi - o la la - sei per pav - ra.

Fuga ad quatuor

Fuge la morie

27

Helas coment
Version A

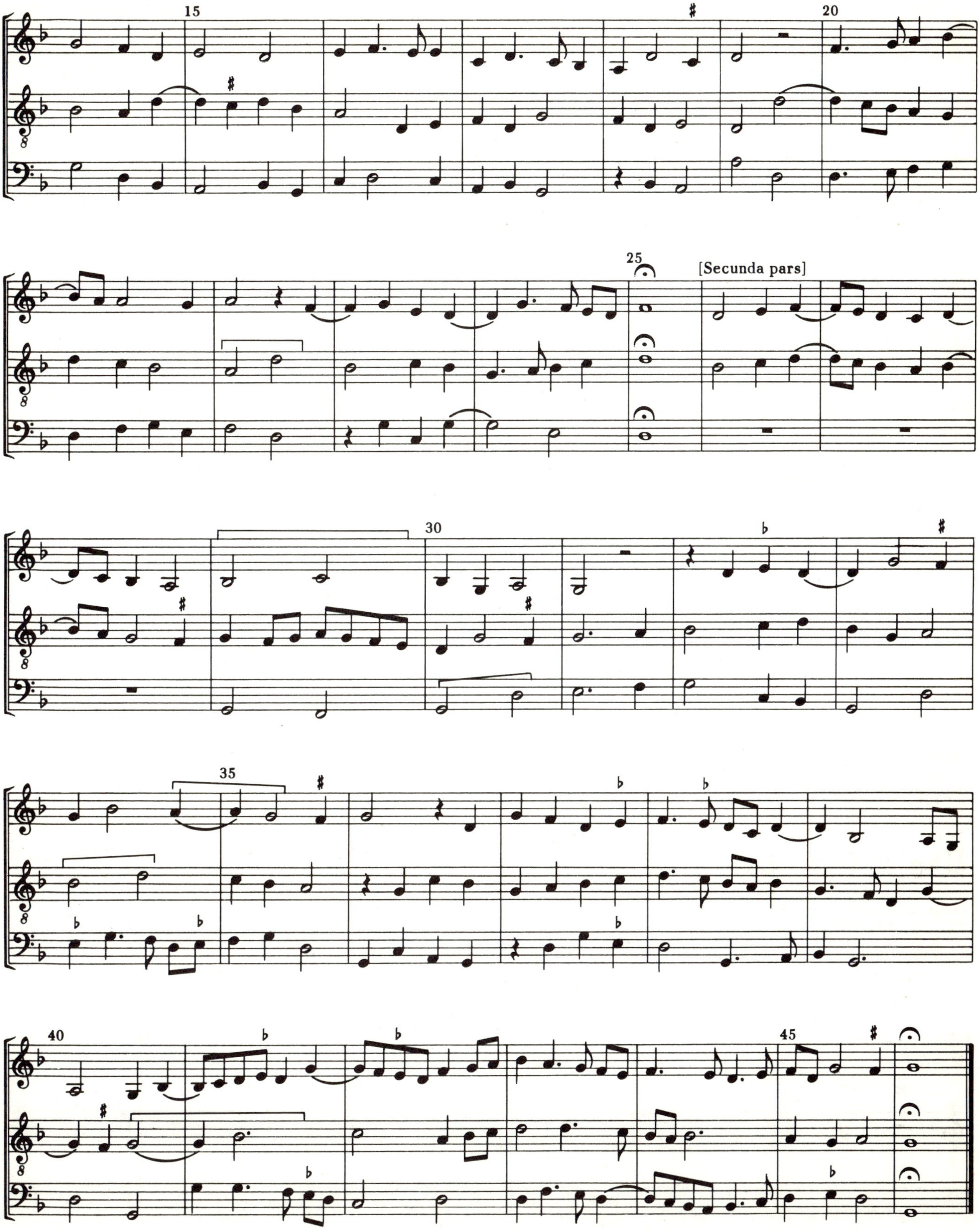
15
20
25
[Secunda pars]
30
35
40
45

Hellas coment anes
Version B

Il est tel

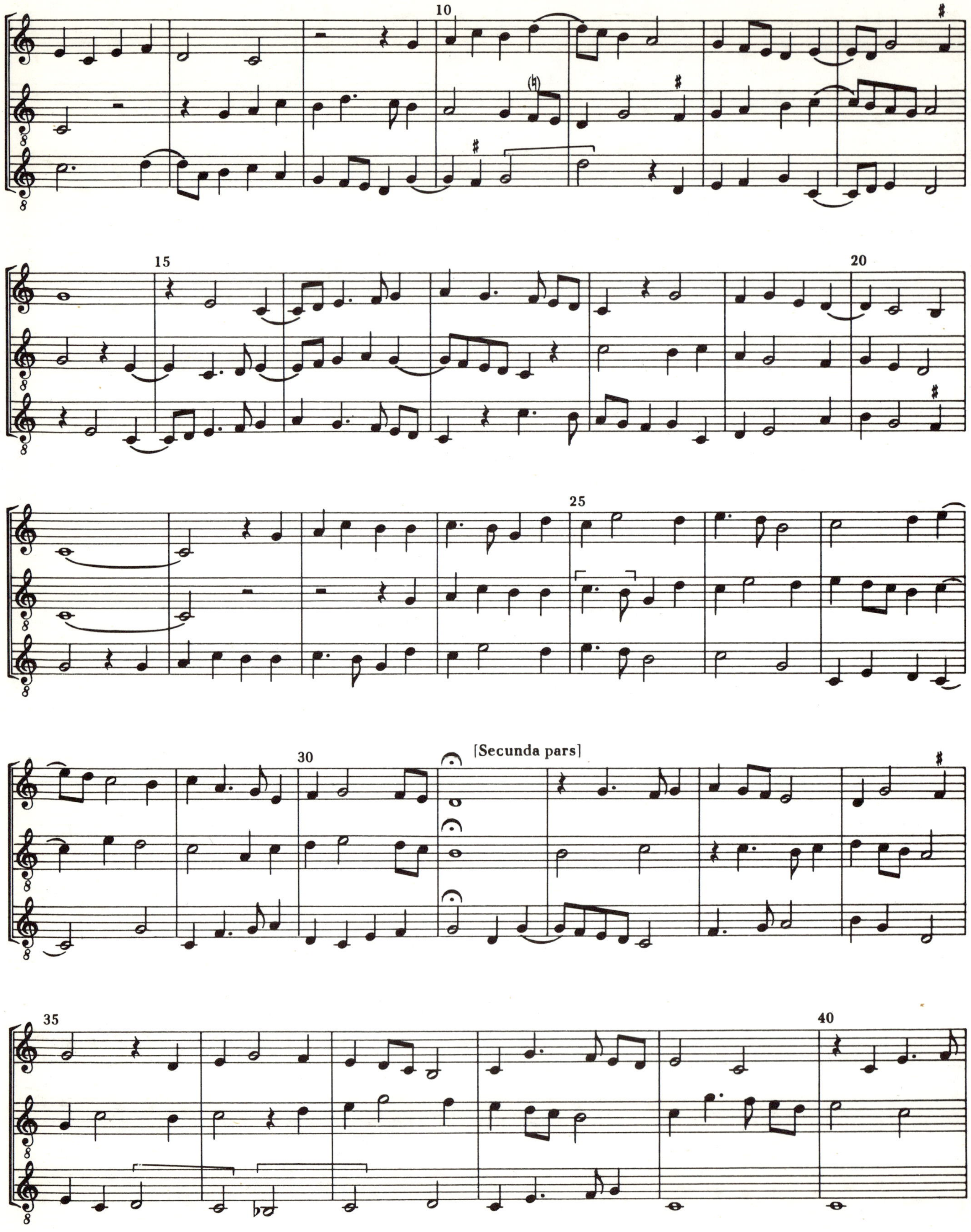
[Secunda pars]

[Il est tousjours]

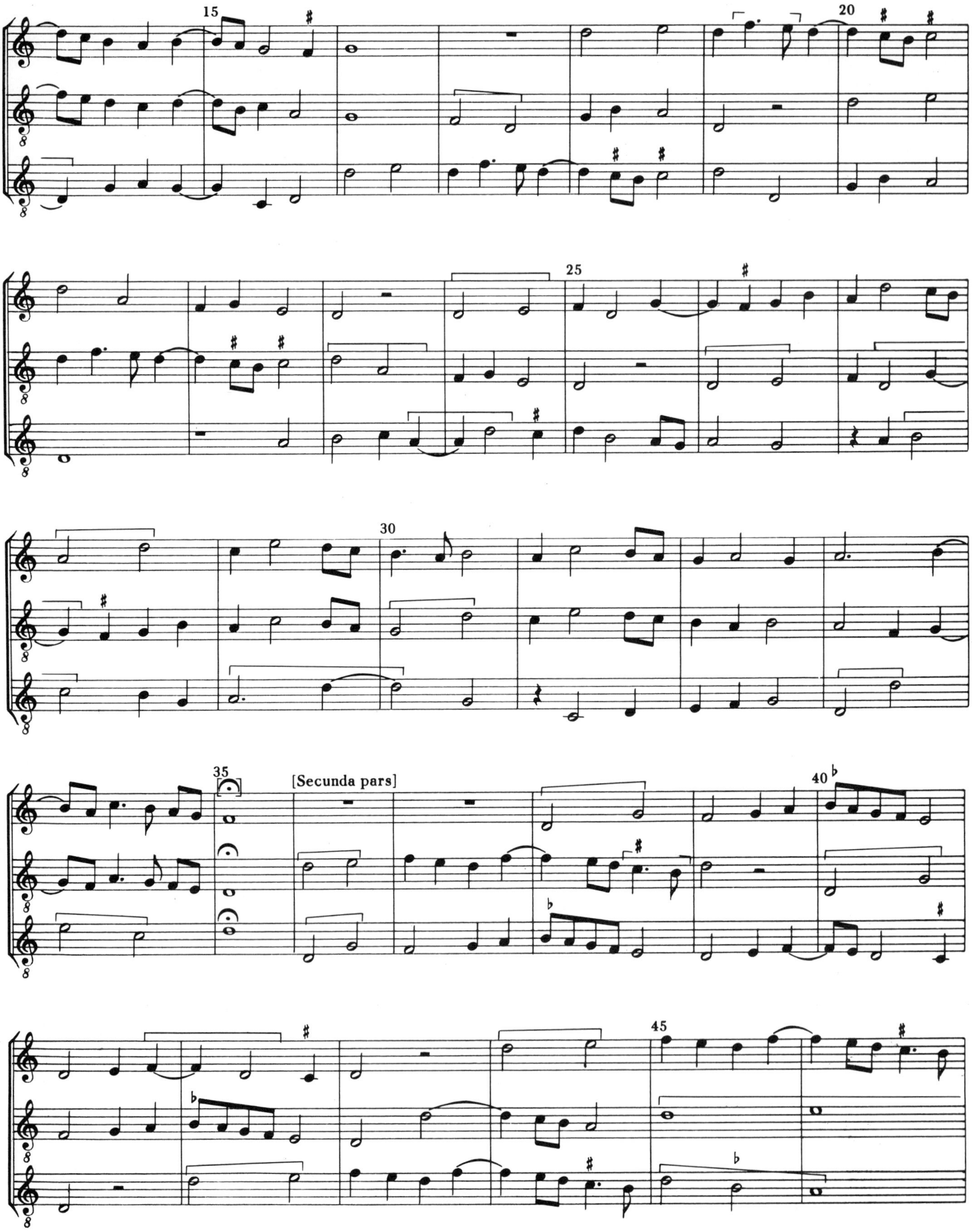
[Secunda pars]

J'ay pris amours
Version A

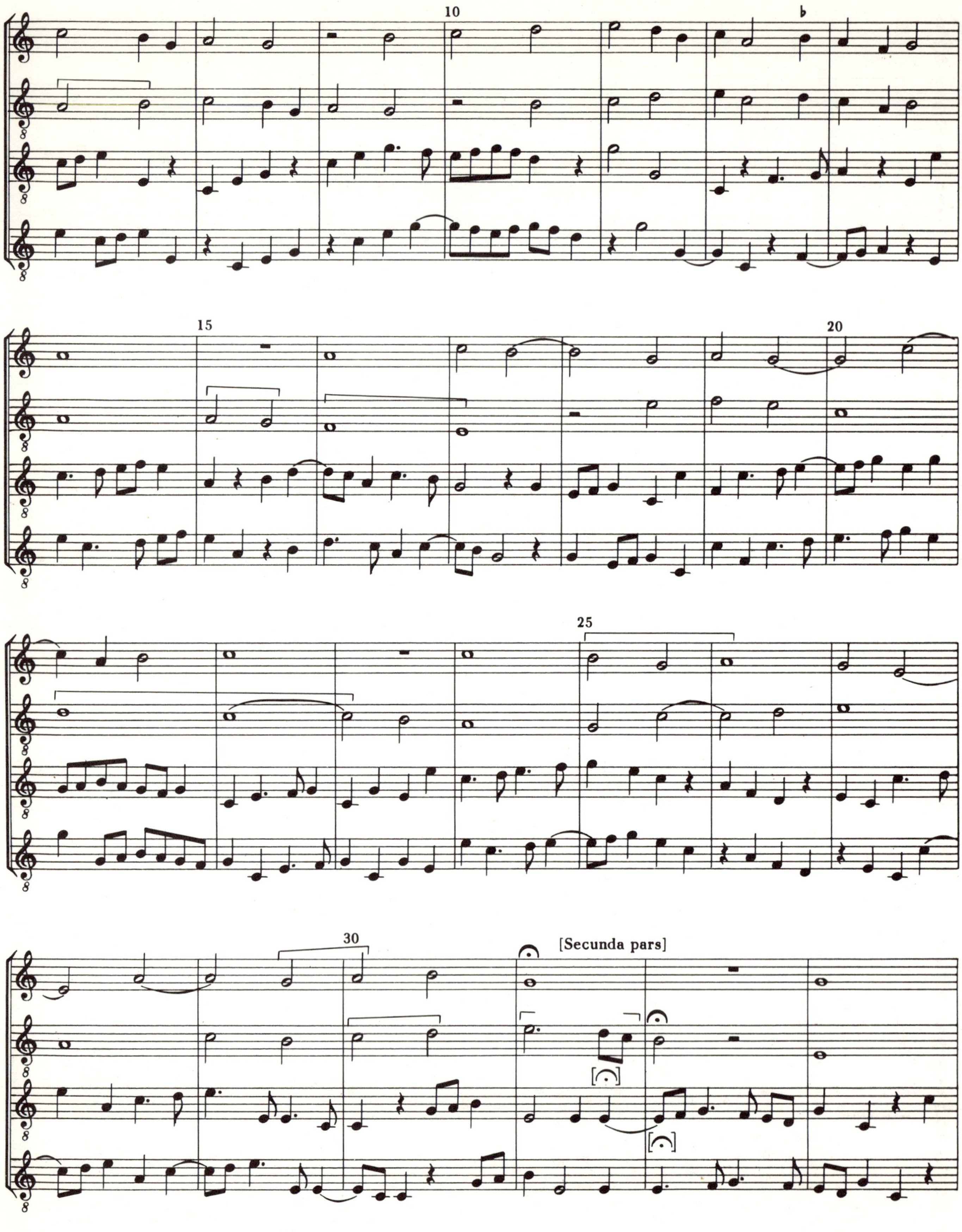
10
15
20
25
30
[Secunda pars]

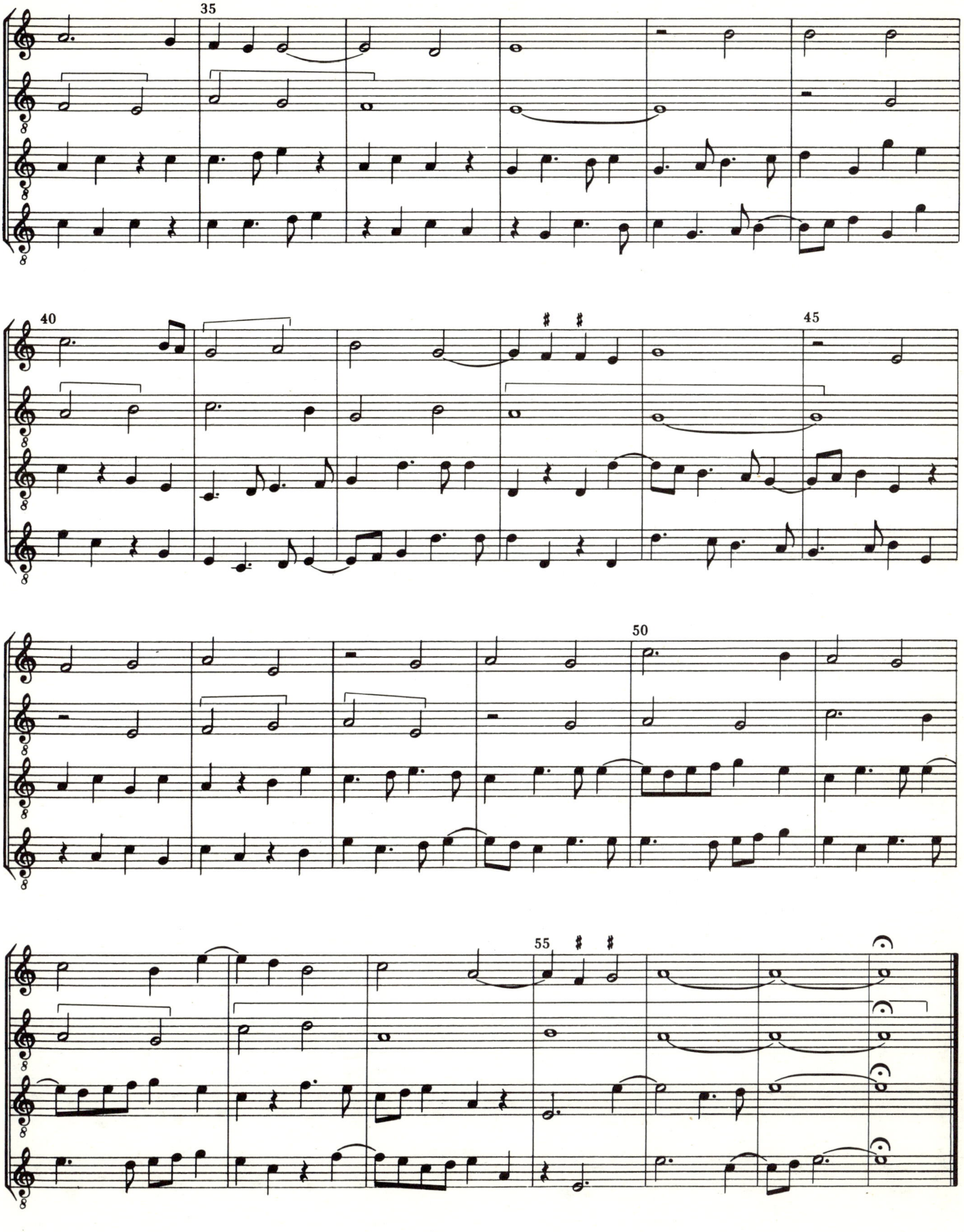
35
40
45
50
55

J'ay pris amours
Version B

25
-té
Eu-
30
- - - reux se- ray le temps d'es-
35
-té Se ve- nir puis à mon
40
45
em- pri- se. S'il est au- -

Je remerchi dieu

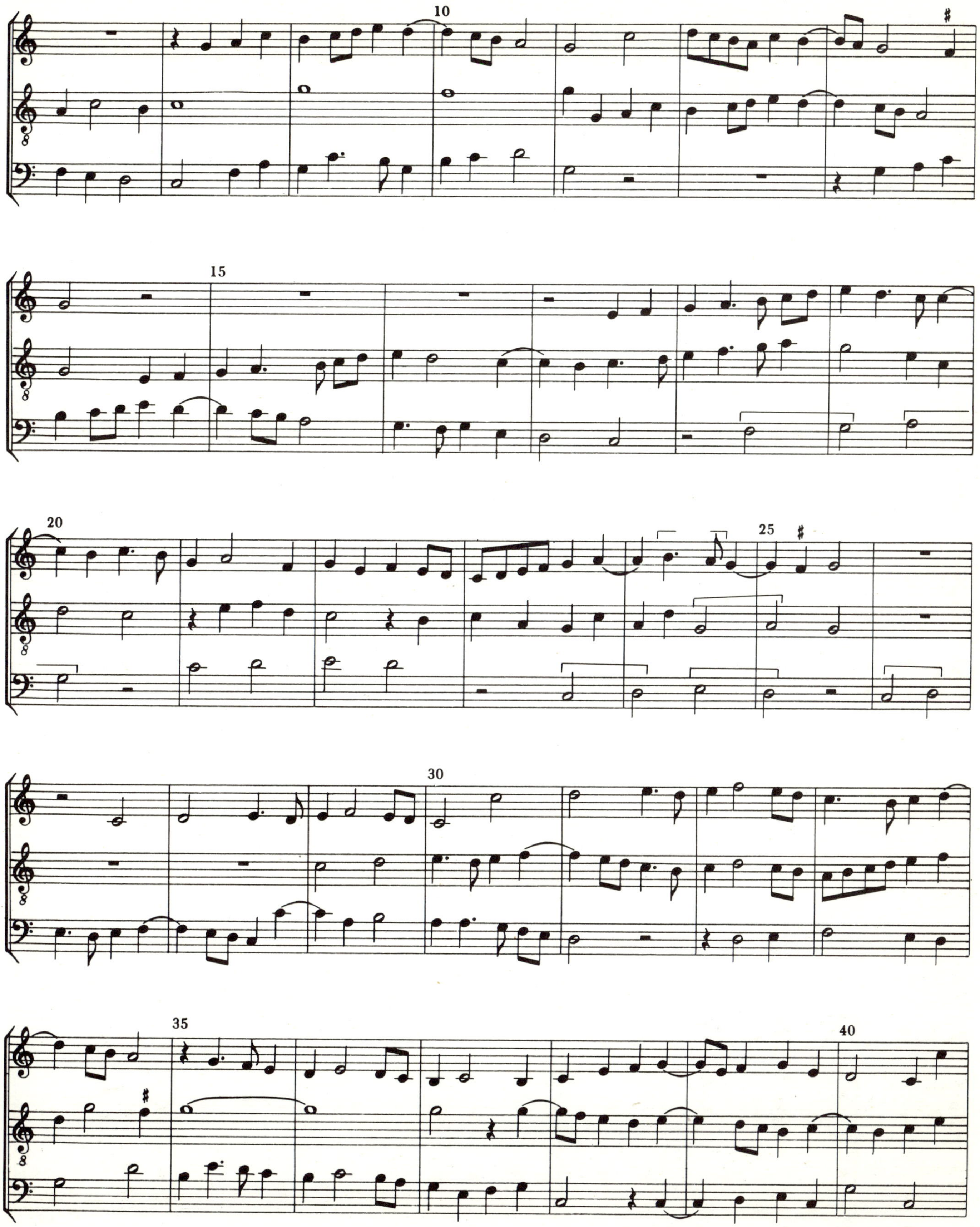
10
15
20
25
30
35
40

J'espoir mieulx

[Secunda pars]

La fleur de biaulte

45

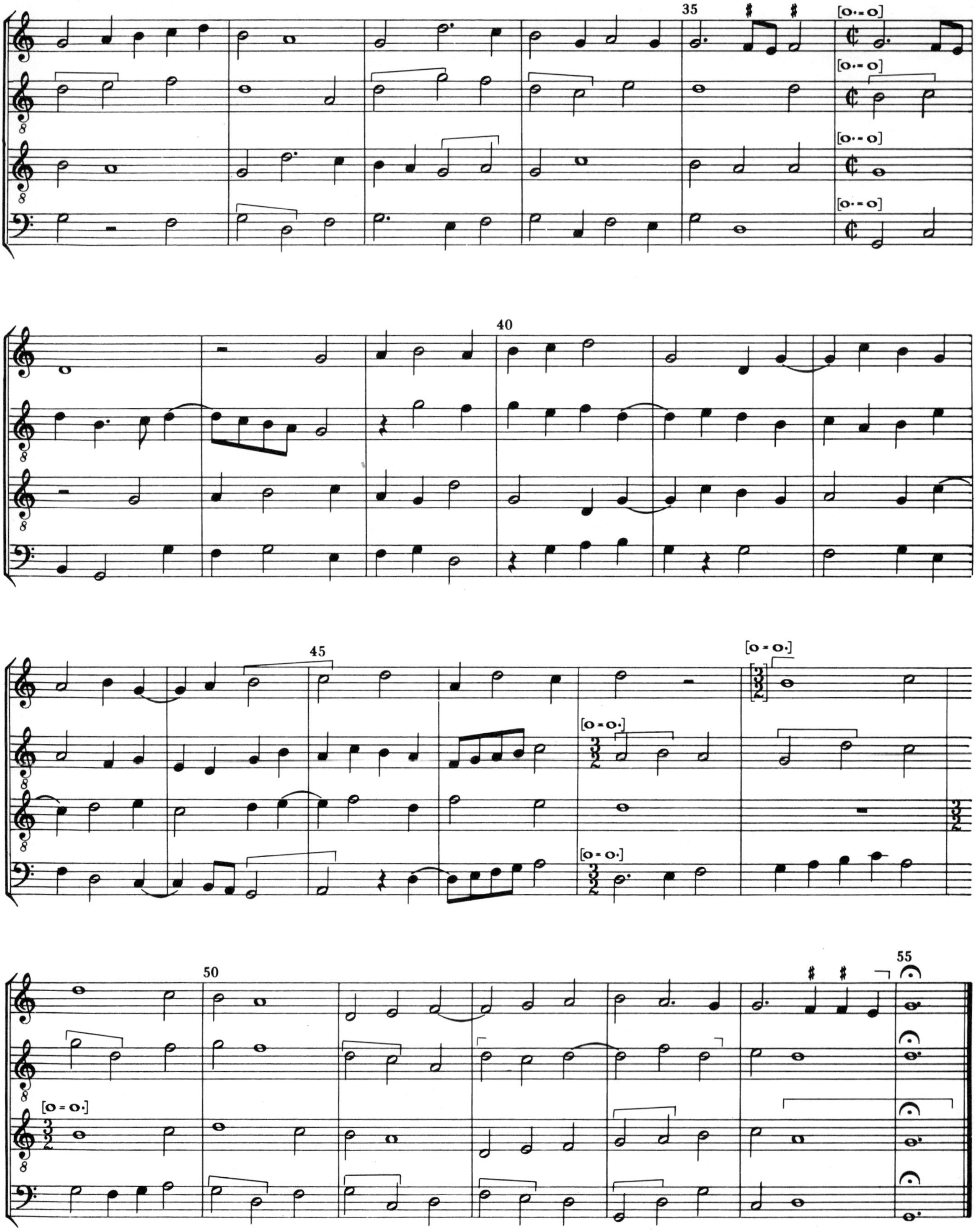
35
[o· = o]
40
45
[o = o·]
50
55

La Martinella

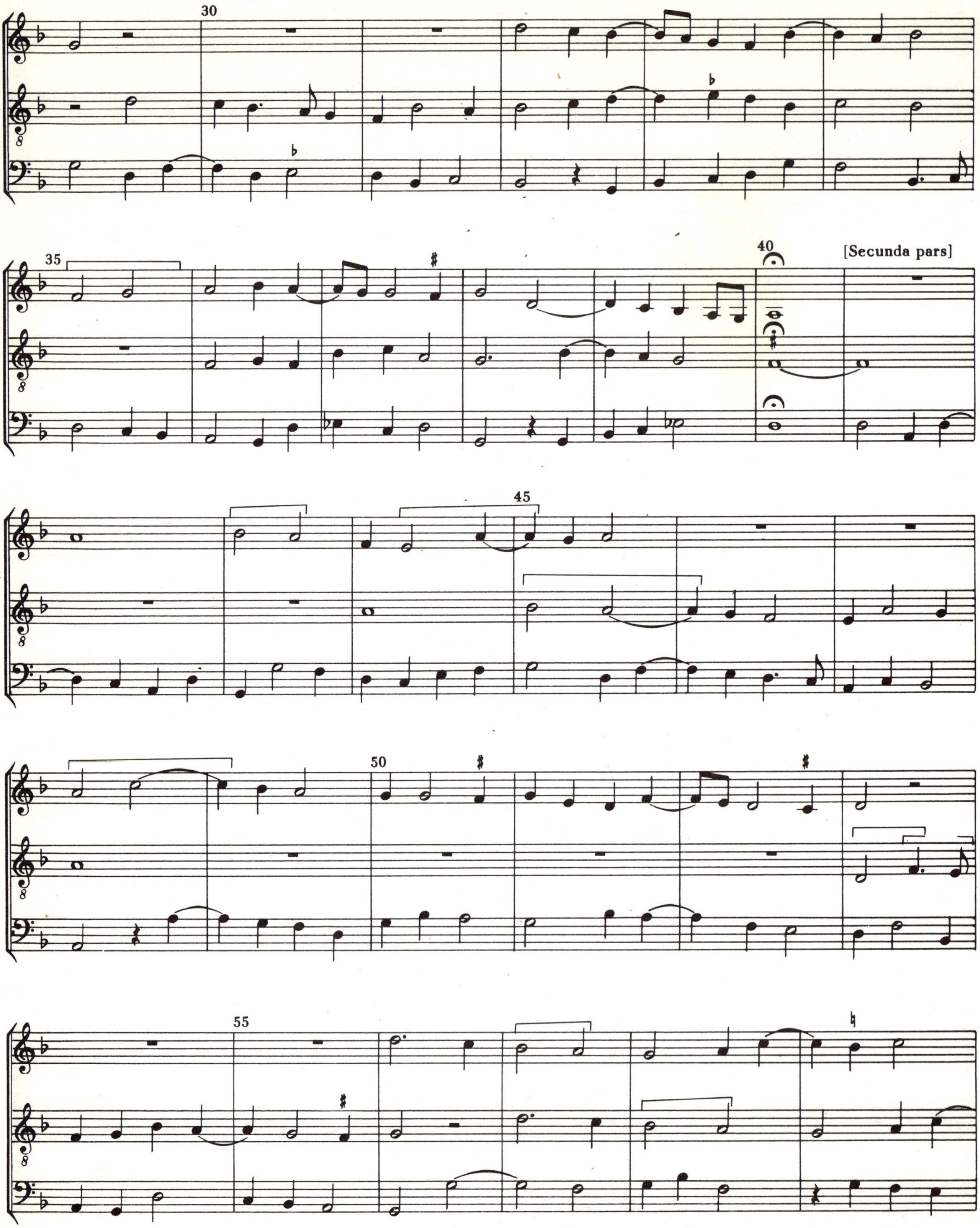
30
35
40
[Secunda pars]
45
50
55

49

La Martinella pittzulo

Le pouverté

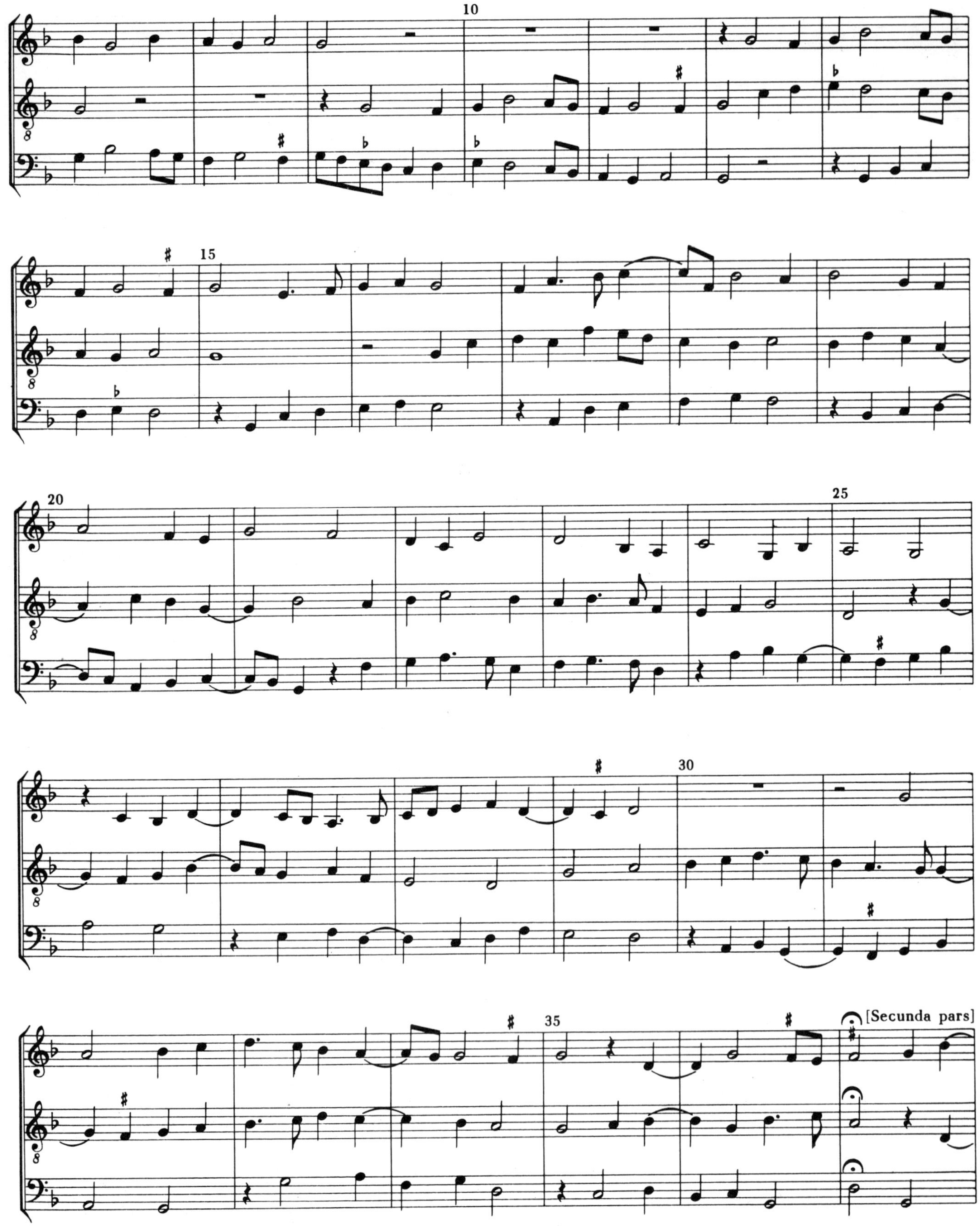
[Secunda pars]

[Malheur me bat]

54

Nenciozza mia

10
Len - chio - - za bal - la - ri - na
15
20
che bal - la um pas - so e me - zo e poy
25
[o = o.]
s'in - chi - na a ri - va - la. De
30
35
ly - vres plains, de ly - - vres plains,

Non per la

Secunda pars

Non seul uno

30 [Secunda pars]

Per faire tousjours

[Cantus]

Tenor

Bassus

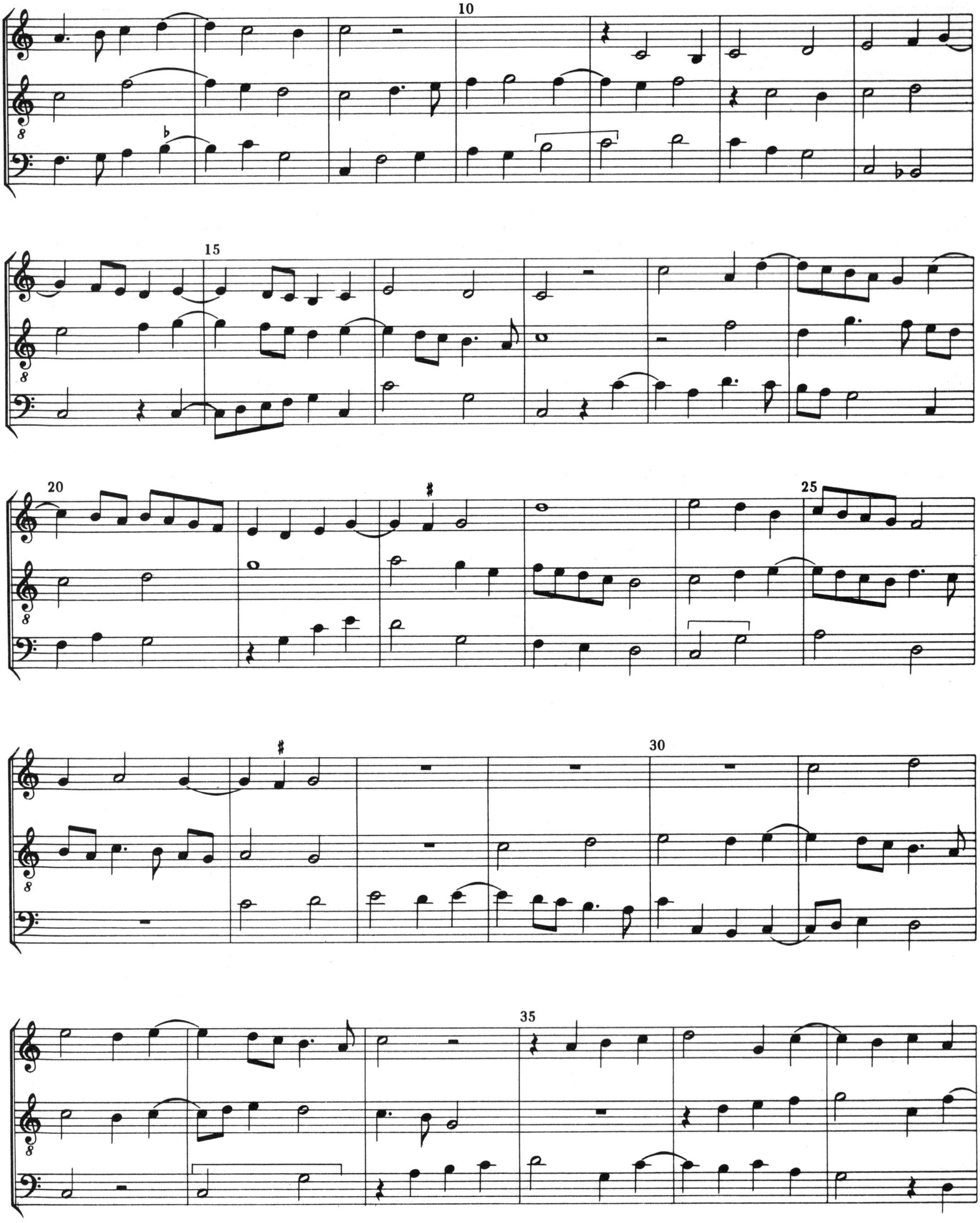
10
15
20
25
30
35

Que je fasoye

Sans siens du mal

65

Tant que dieu vosdra

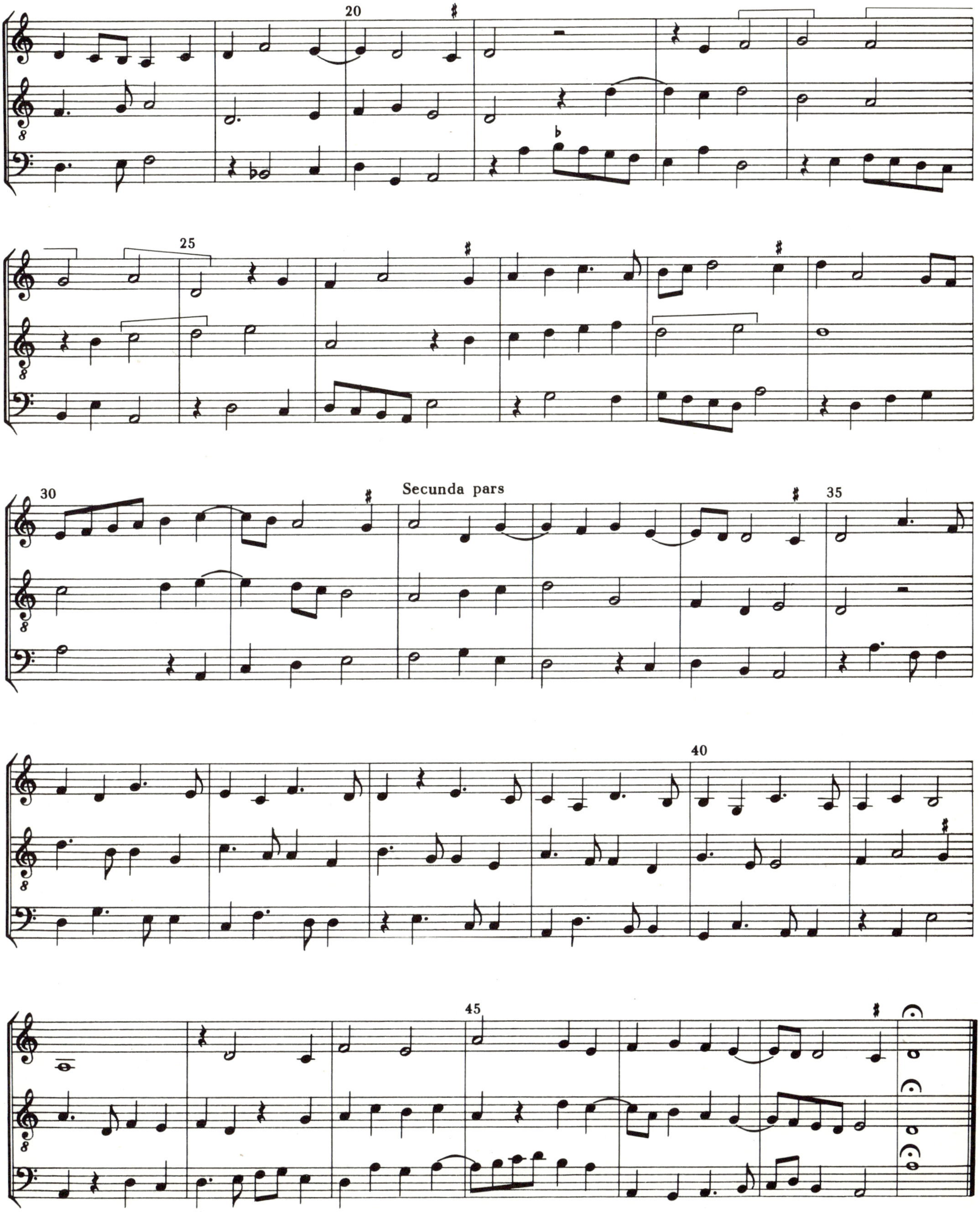
20
25
30
Secunda pars
35
40
45

Tousjours bien

[Secunda pars]

Tousjours me souviendra

Tout joyeulx

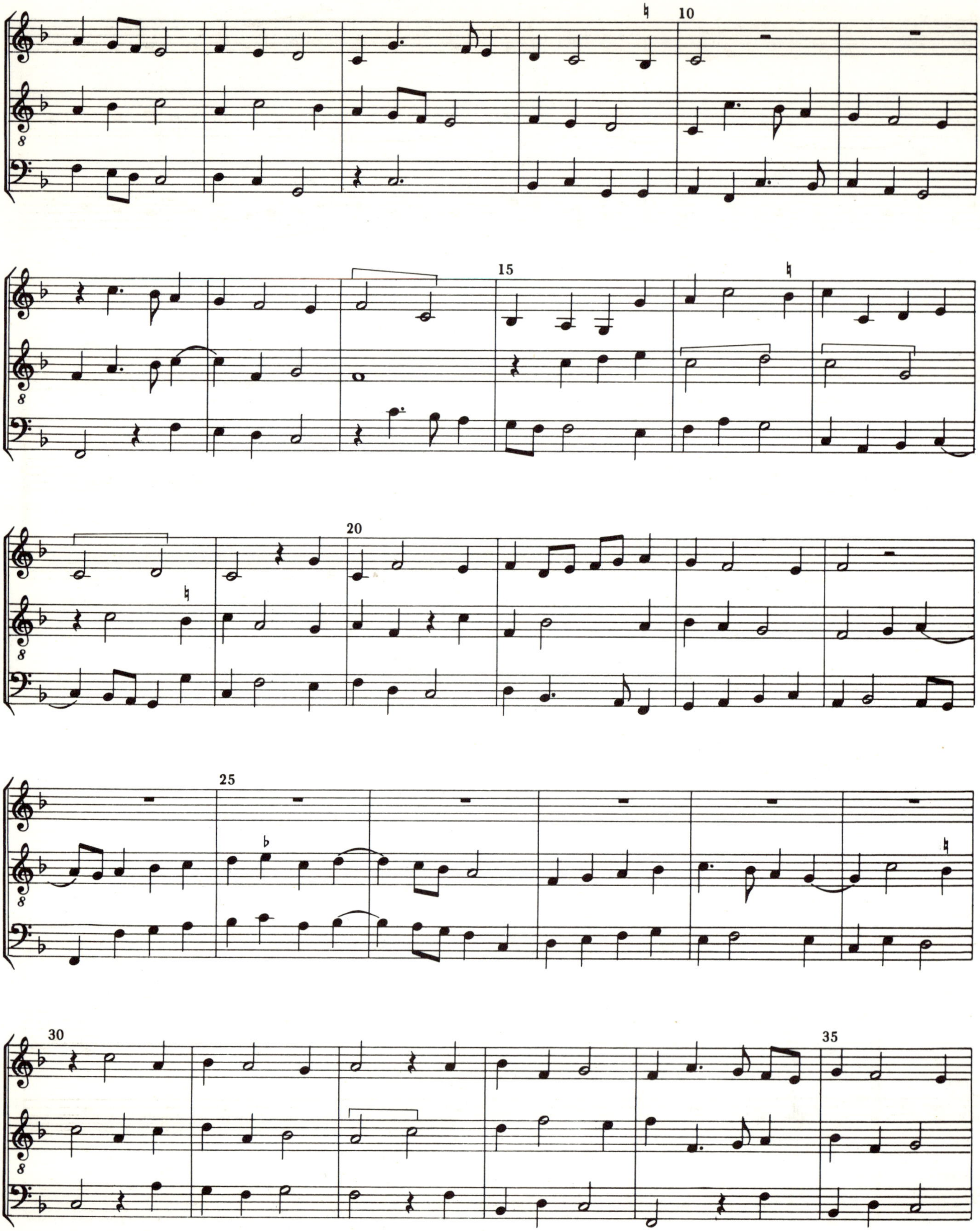
10
15
20
25
30
35

Tres doulx regart

74

Vive, vive

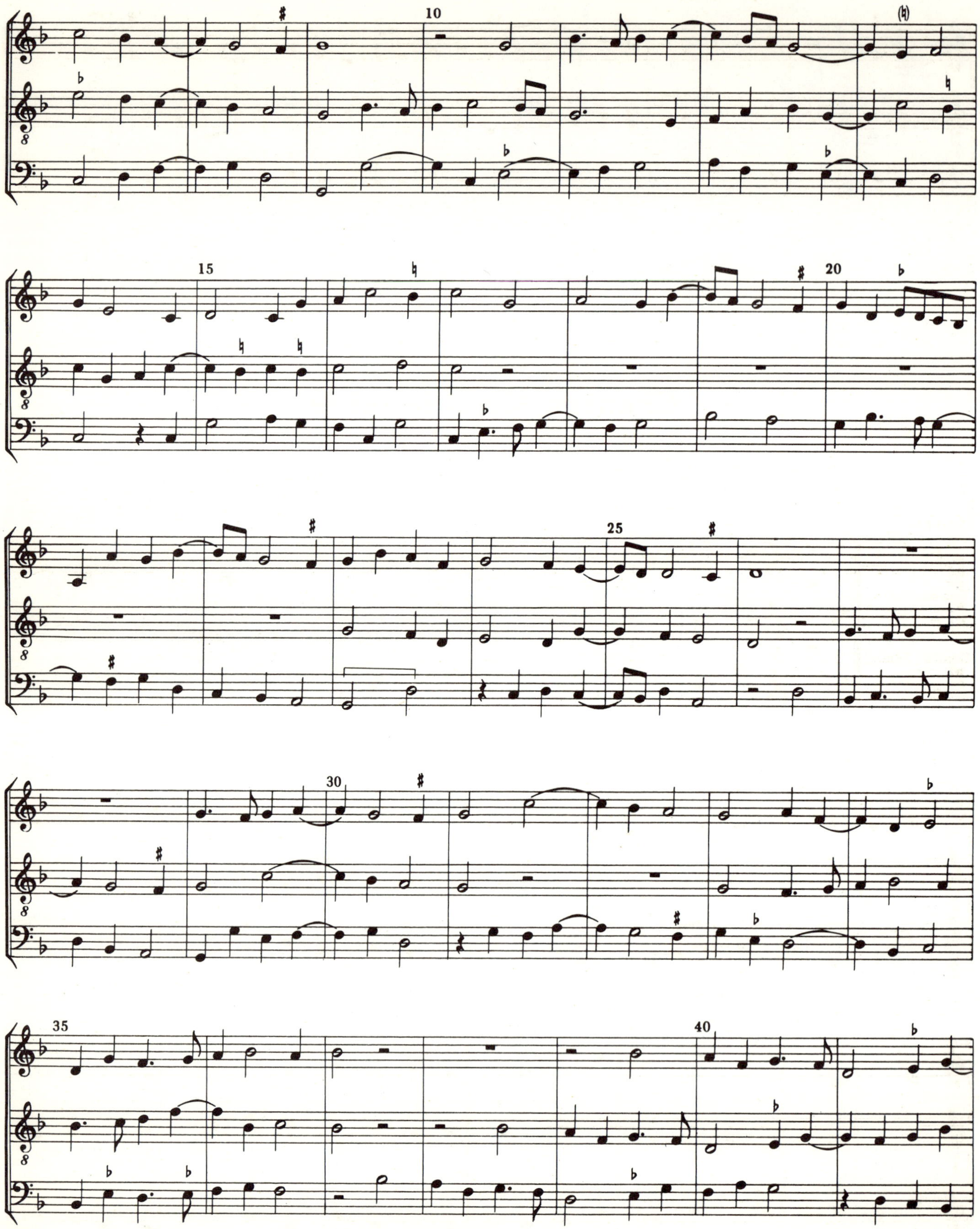
10
15
20
25
30
35
40

Chanson "do si la sol la"

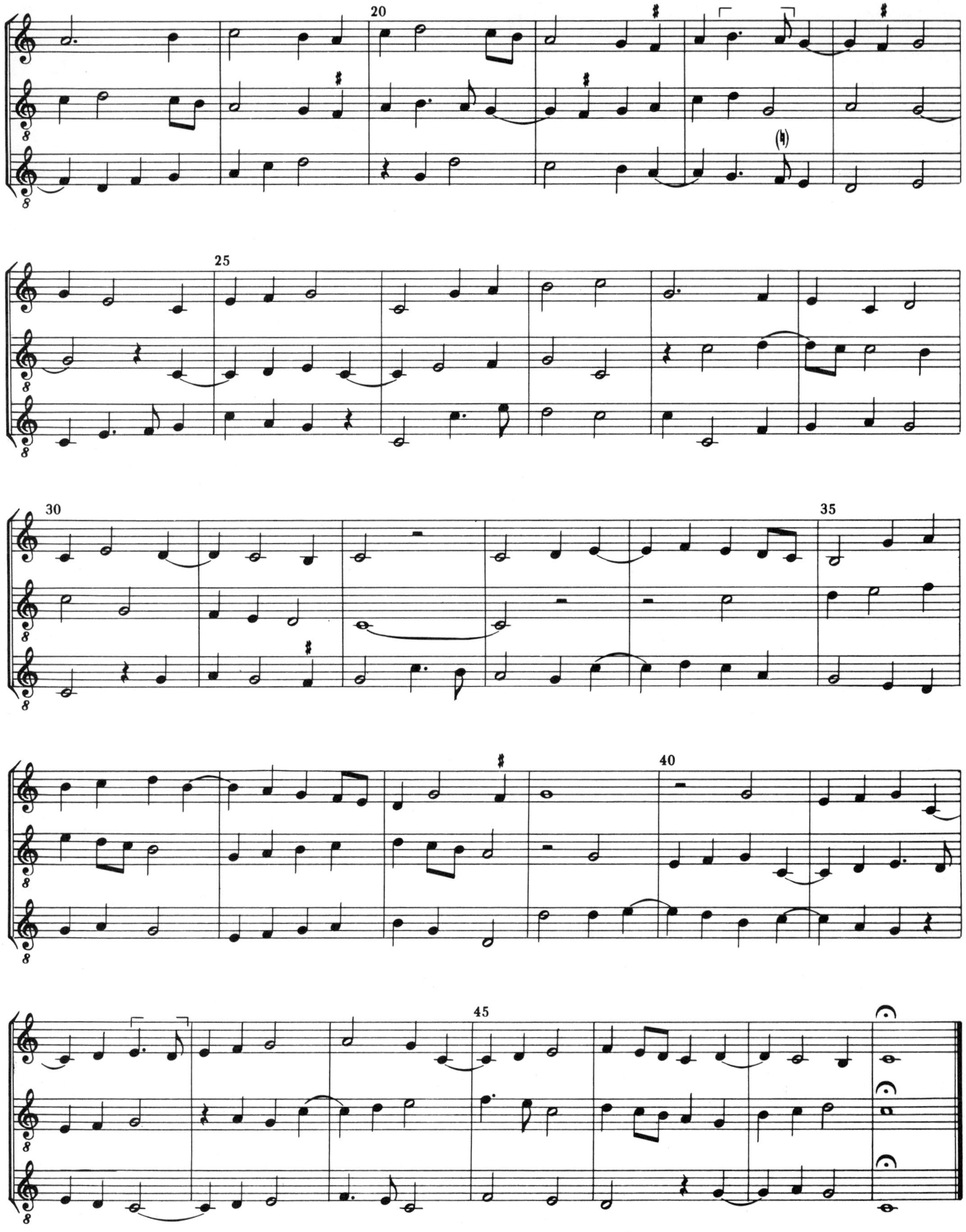
20
25
30
35
40
45

Chanson "Re mi fa sol la"

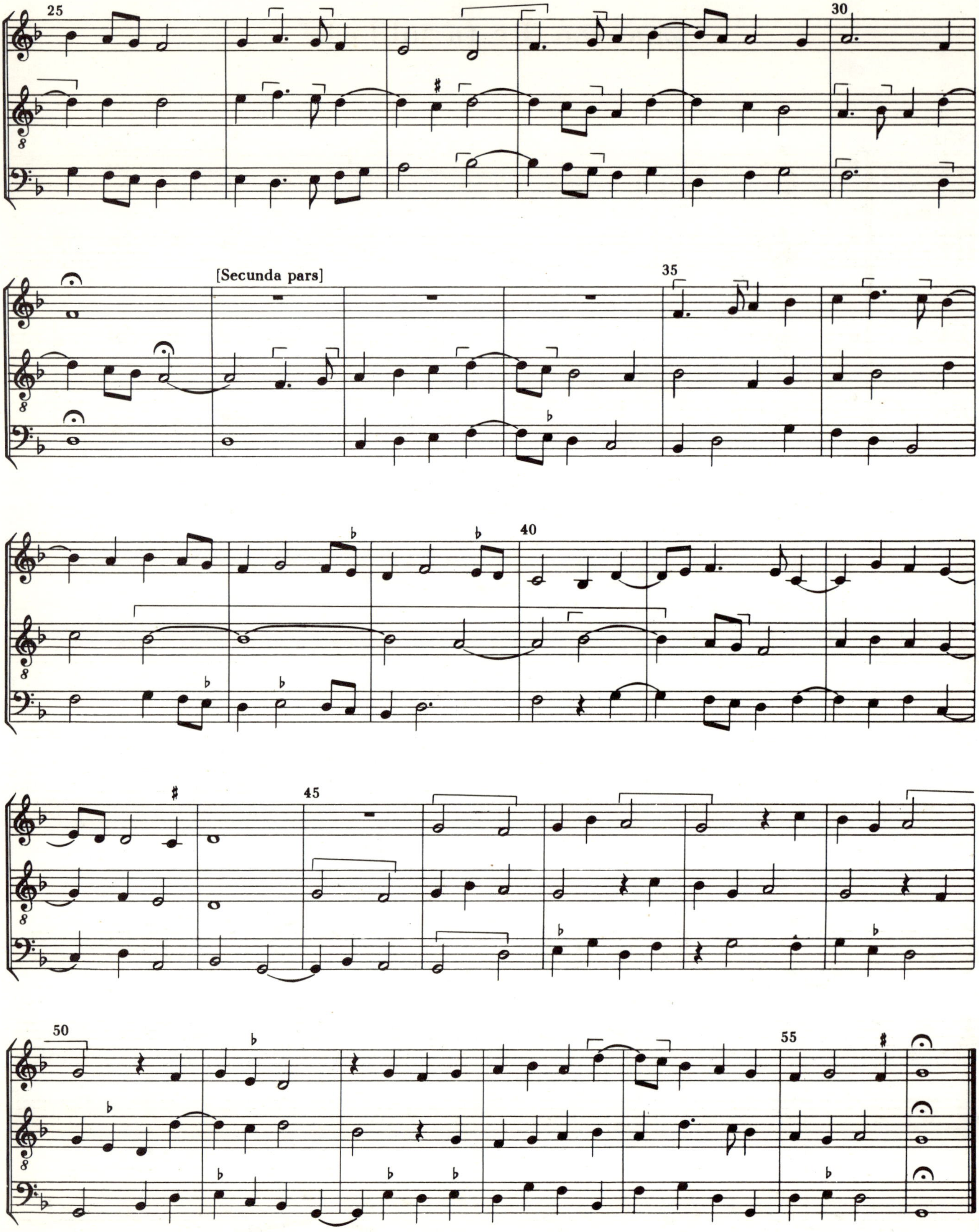
25
30
[Secunda pars]
35
40
45
50
55

Chanson "Re fa sol la la"

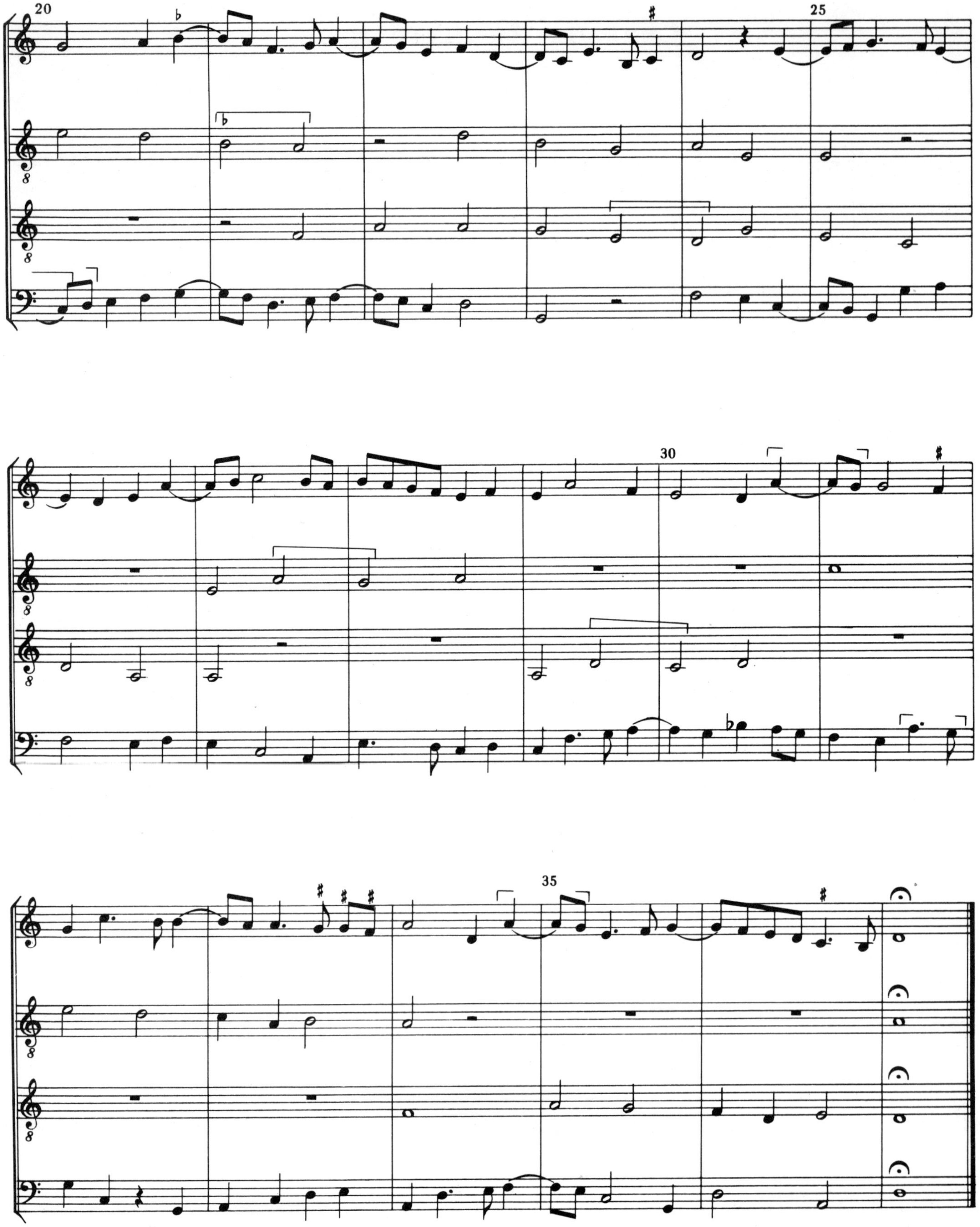
20
25
30
35

Chanson "Fa mi re do re"

84

Chanson "Sol mi fa sol sol"

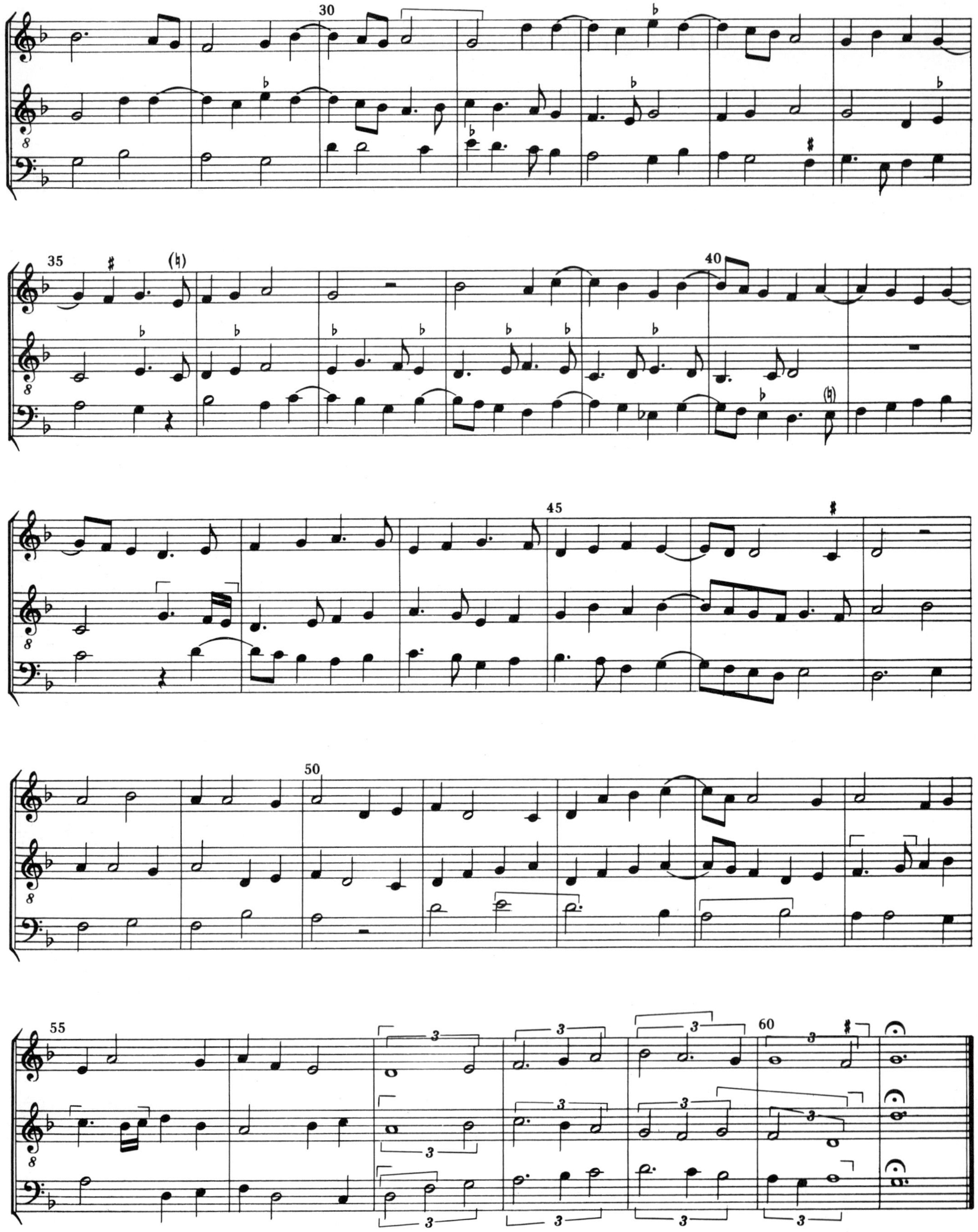

Chanson "Sol fa mi fa sol"

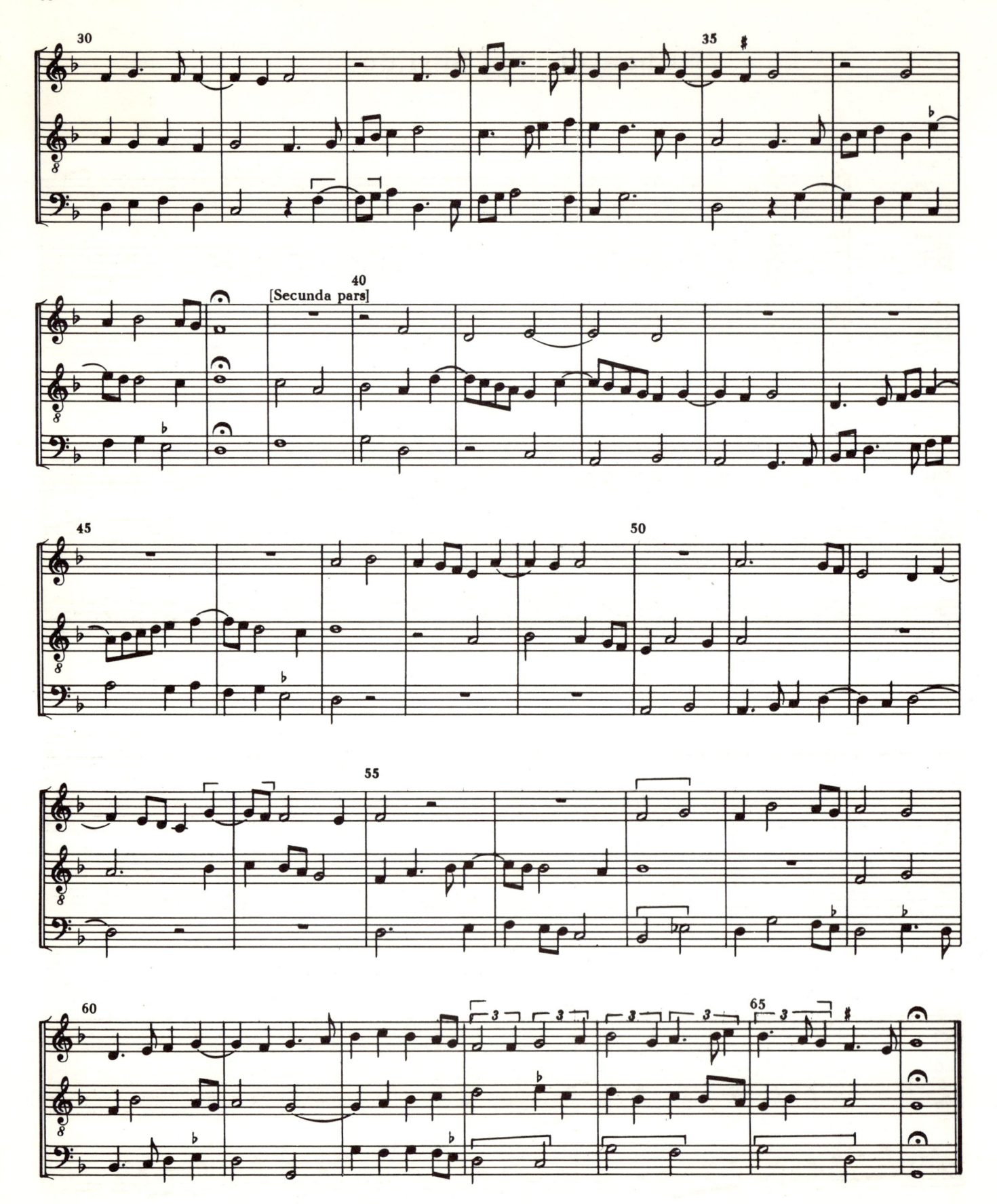
30
35
40
[Secunda pars]
45
50
55
60
65

Chanson "Sol la si do si"

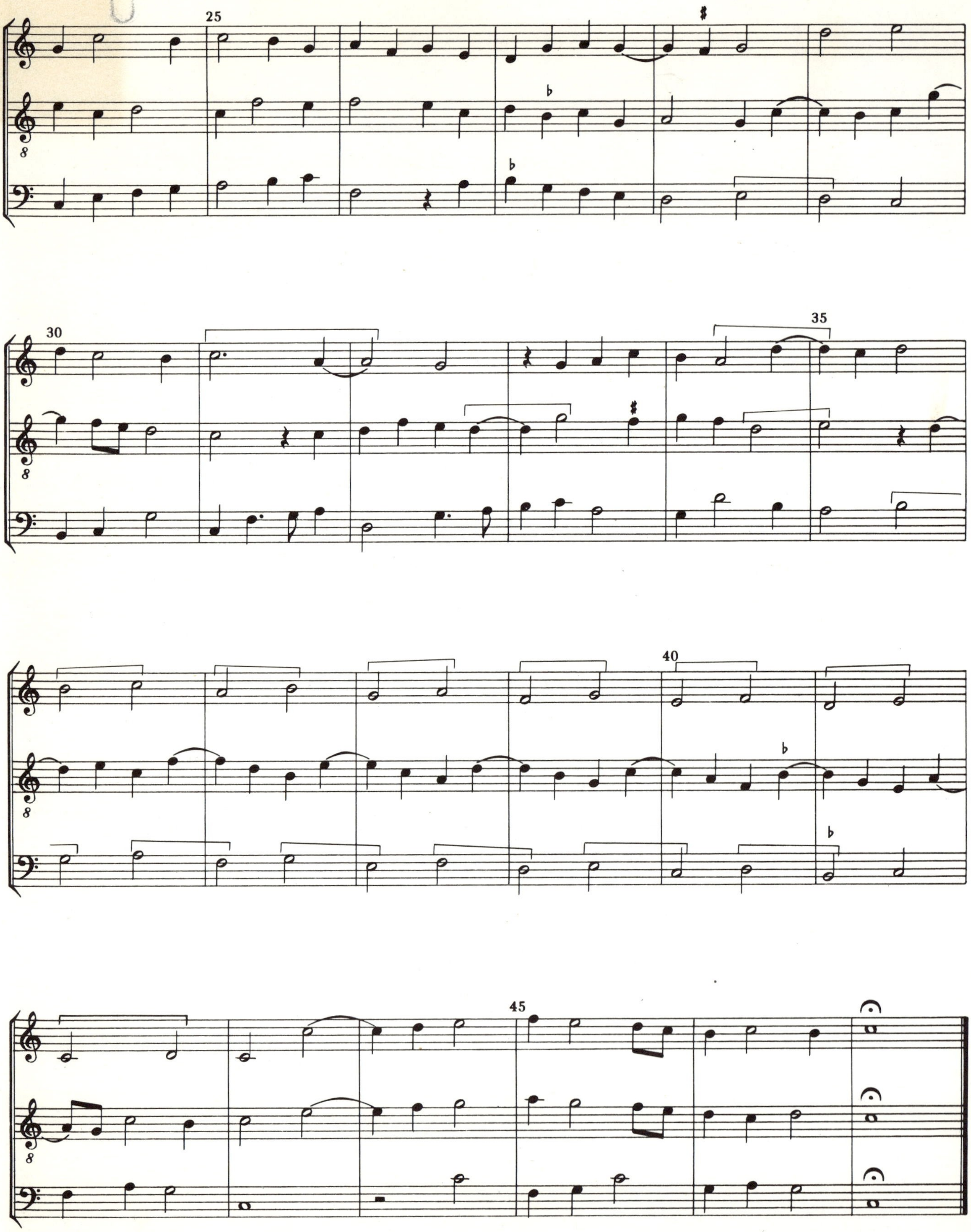
25
30
35
40
45